Harnessing Outsourcing
for Business Advantage

Financial Times Management Briefings are happy to receive proposals from individuals who have expertise in the field of management education.

If you would like to discuss your ideas further, please contact Andrew Mould, Commissioning Editor.

Tel: 0171 447 2210
Fax: 0171 240 5771
e-mail: andrew.mould@ftmanagement.com

MANAGEMENT BRIEFINGS

GENERAL MANAGEMENT

Harnessing Outsourcing for Business Advantage

IAN LAW

FINANCIAL TIMES

MANAGEMENT

LONDON · SAN FRANCISCO
KUALA LUMPUR · JOHANNESBURG

*Financial Times Management delivers the knowledge,
skills and understanding that enable students,
managers and organisations to achieve their ambitions,
whatever their needs, wherever they are.*

London Office:
128 Long Acre, London WC2E 9AN
Tel: +44 (0)171 447 2000
Fax: +44 (0)171 240 5771
Website: www.ftmanagement.com

A Division of Financial Times Professional Limited

First published in Great Britain 1999

ISBN 0 273 63723 1

British Library Cataloguing in Publication Data
A CIP catalogue record for this book can be obtained from the British Library.

10 9 8 7 6 5 4 3 2 1

Typeset by Boyd Elliott Typesetting
Printed and bound in Great Britain

The Publishers' policy is to use paper manufactured from sustainable forests.

About the author

Ian Law is a Principal Consultant at KPMG Management Consulting in London, where he is a practice leader in the firm's outsourcing advisory practice which assists organisations with outsourcing issues. His work has focused on assessing outsourcing options for clients and in managing the implementation of the chosen option. His client portfolio to date includes both public and private sector organisations. His private sector client base is largely retail, FMCG and financial services organisations. Within KPMG Ian has business and service development responsibilities.

He has a BSc in Computer Science from University College Cork and an MBA from Cranfield School of Management. He is a frequent speaker at conferences in Europe, the USA, South Africa and South East Asia on service level agreements and outsourcing.

Ian can be contacted on the internet: Ian.Law@KPMG.co.uk

Contents

Acknowledgements

This book is the product of the efforts of a number of people whose contribution I wish to acknowledge. I am grateful to my colleagues at KPMG Consulting for providing the support and opportunities which led to this book. Very special thanks to Mitchell Stamp and Deborah Houser for reviewing some of the chapters and for their valuable comments and suggestions. I am indebted to Graham Nixon, my managing partner, for his encouragement and sponsorship throughout this venture. Finally, to Sandra, my deepest gratitude for the precious free time she sacrificed to help me with this book.

Preface

Those of us who have chosen to make outsourcing our field of expertise are retained because we have experienced outsourcing first hand, many times. We do not understand all of the risks, issues and pitfalls of outsourcing because nobody does. However, we do know most of them. This is the value we bring to organisations. The risks and issues covered and the hints and tips contained in this book are the product of that experience.

The assertions and recommendations made in this book are based on my understanding of the outsourcing business. Much of that understanding has been acquired directly by assisting organisations, both the buyers and suppliers of outsourced services, through various phases of the outsourcing process. The rest comes from a distillation of the thousands of cases and anecdotes related to me by buyers, suppliers, consultants and lawyers.

Like all disciplines, outsourcing has developed its own terminology. The outsourcing terms in this book are not likely to be new to the reader but the precise meaning of the terms in the context of outsourcing might be. All of these terms are explained briefly in the glossary and usually also when they first occur in the text.

The importance of the outsourcing contract which binds buyer and supplier cannot be stressed enough. This book refers to the outsourcing contract in several places and particularly throughout Chapter 6. Where a comment or recommendation is made with regard to a specific legal point I make it as a layman and it is intended purely as a guide for the reader. The validity and ramification of these points within the context of a specific outsourcing deal can only be assessed by the lawyers and others involved in that deal. What these points should highlight is the importance of the legal advice which lawyers with specific outsourcing expertise can provide.

This book is unquestionably biased towards the perspective of the buyer of outsourced services. This is principally because suppliers generally have the experience of many outsourcing deals and are usually considerably more informed than their clients when deals are being made. One of the objectives of this book is to redress this balance by raising the buyer's awareness of outsourcing issues and risks.

Introduction

The transformation in business thinking over the past twenty to thirty years has been dramatic. Many organisations have accepted that in today's world they must be excellent at what they do and that excellence can best be achieved by focusing on a few specific activities. It is with this rationale that so many of the world's organisations have embarked in recent years on an unprecedented number of company disposals, acquisitions and mergers and on the redefinition of the traditional supply chain. But this need to focus goes beyond these corporate reorganisations and challenges organisations to demonstrate excellence in their own support activities, such as finance, human resources and information technology. Where these activities (or parts of them) fall outside of the company's 'excellence focus' they are euphemistically labelled 'non-core' and are outsourced to another organisation whose skill it is to manage and operate them.

Outsourcing – the provision by third parties of services previously supplied in house – has flourished in recent years. Outsource providers have matured from being the custodians of organisations' data centres to delivering a wide range of financial, procurement, human resources and technology services – to mention but a few. Organisations are revising their strategies and outsourcing is becoming the most commonly used tool to implement new strategies. It is unquestionably here to stay. Not to consider outsourcing is to put the future of an organisation at risk.

However, corporate decision makers also put organisations at risk when they choose to outsource. Surveys of organisations in outsourcing deals unveil concerns about supplier inflexibility, rising rather than falling supplier charges and failed expectations. Outsourcing's potential high rewards are shadowed by high risks – shadows not often noticed in the glare of the potential rewards. Tales of deals 'gone wrong' abound – suppliers acquired by their clients' competitors, strategic mismatches between supplier and buyer, unexpected supplier charges and poor performance. Also, reversing the decision is costly – and in some cases impossible. If outsourcing is to be used then it must be used carefully. To ignore the risks is reckless.

The aim of this book is to lead decision makers through the outsourcing minefield. It assumes that these decision makers have limited time to give to the outsourcing process, but that they are ultimately accountable for the outcome of the process and therefore need to be fully briefed. Where applicable, common or standard practice is described to aid the decision maker's understanding. This book is not, however, intended to be an in-depth guide to the outsourcing process but rather a discussion about frequently encountered outsourcing issues and risks and a guide to some of the arguments which surround the critical decisions in an outsourcing deal.

The approach taken in this book is to consider the key risks that outsourcing poses to an organisation. Methods for reducing or even removing these risks are recommended. This book is structured around a series of outsourcing recommendations aimed at reducing organisations' exposure to outsourcing risks. Each chapter discusses the risks, issues and options in relation to that particular recommendation. The principal recommendations are:

- Chapter 2: *Understand the outsourcing process*
- Chapter 3: *Put an effective outsourcing team in place*
- Chapter 4: *Evaluate the case for outsourcing*
- Chapter 5: *Select the best supplier*
- Chapter 6: *Build a robust outsourcing contract*
- Chapter 8: *Create strong service level agreements*
- Chapter 9: *Manage the outsourcing contract effectively*
- Chapter 10: *Be prepared for contract termination*.

Additionally, Chapter 1 provides an overview of outsourcing and Chapter 7 examines the issues surrounding the pricing of outsourcing deals and the structuring of bonus and penalty regimes in outsourcing contracts.

For corporate decision makers faced with having to consider and/or implement an outsourcing transaction, then this book is essential.

Outsourcing – an overview

Introduction

Outsourcing is a fluid concept which has developed rapidly during its relatively brief existence. To avoid confusion over what is meant by this often misused term, the starting point of this chapter is a short description of what is generally understood by 'outsourcing'. It is also important to understand how the outsourcing market has developed, since an understanding of the historical perspective enables a company considering the outsourcing option to take advantage of lessons learned in the past. Next the key risks and benefits of an outsourcing deal are assessed, along with a consideration of what can realistically be outsourced. Finally, a brief look is taken at what the future holds for outsourcing.

A definition of outsourcing

A typical outsourcing transaction will consist of two parts. First, there is the transfer to a third party of the responsibility for the operation and management of part of an organisation. This will often include the transfer to the supplier of some or all of the assets (including staff) which comprise that part of the organisation. Second, there is the provision of services to the organisation by the supplier, usually for a period of several years. By way of example consider a payroll department. The buyer transfers the payroll clerks, consumables, computer systems, procedural documentation and the computer operations staff to the supplier. The supplier in return provides the buyer with specific payroll services such as the production and delivery of payslips on a weekly or monthly basis.

The first stage – the transfer of assets from buyer to supplier – usually comprises the transfer of staff, computers and other hardware (owned or leased), software (owned or licensed), other third-party contracts, e.g. supply agreements in relation to consumables, intellectual property rights and access to, or other rights in, property. The buyer will often expect the supplier to purchase its assets such as computer hardware. However, suppliers are not bound to take on assets from a buyer and indeed some supplier organisations will refuse to accept some or all assets. In this scenario the assets are not transferred but the buyer grants the supplier use of the assets for the term of the contract.

The historical perspective

It is important to understand why so many organisations outsource – or in the words of the critics – 'sell the crown jewels'.

Fundamental to outsourcing is the belief that an organisation would benefit from a third party taking responsibility for some of its internal functions or processes rather than retaining that responsibility itself. Thus in the 1980s organisations contracted with third-party organisations to manage their facilities. The objective of this temporary third-party management team was to increase the efficiency and effectiveness of the managed function but for control to be retained by the buyer. Usually staff and all other assets were retained by the buyer. This type of contract management deal is often referred to as facilities management (FM).[1] An FM provider was essentially a contracted line manager.

It is difficult to draw a clear line between FM and outsourcing. For simplicity it is easiest to regard FM, as its title suggests, as a management contract (even if it involves a limited transfer of assets to the supplier). The buyer pays the supplier a management charge which is essentially a flat fee which is not tied to business performance. As the FM provider gained more day-to-day exposure to the buyer's organisation its role soon expanded to include an advisory role. While the buyer no longer managed the relevant function it still retained responsibility for the assets, including staff, which comprised that function. Without day-to-day contact with the function this became more cumbersome. Inevitably it made sense for the buyer to consider also transferring these residual responsibilities to the supplier.

The origin of outsourcing is generally accepted to be in information technology (IT). In the 1980s, organisations, initially in the US, expanded the FM concept of the supplier managing a function (for which it received a straight management charge) to include additionally supplier responsibility for the ownership and operation of the function (with a commensurate change in the charging structure to reflect the increase in the supplier's roles and responsibilities). This occurred at a time when the IT function of many medium-sized to large organisations comprised large mainframe data centres. The senior management of these organisations often understood very little about these data processing systems and watched in amazement as millions of corporate dollars 'disappeared' into the IT department each year. And, because the IT function was

---

1. Facilities management is also used to denote the management of a building such as an office block.

generally not represented at board level, senior executives began to doubt the efficacy of their own IT management, which now received a significant amount of the organisation's annual spend.

Outsource providers – of which there were very few in the mid-1980s compared with today – offered senior executives a solution. They would take over the management and operation of these data centre facilities for which they would pay the organisation the market value of the assets. In return the buyer would pay a monthly or quarterly charge to the supplier which was usually less than the in-house cost of running the data centre. Additionally, the supplier would often commit to reducing the charge year on year over the life of the deal, typically five to ten years.

Suppliers were in a position to make this commitment for several reasons:

1   their involvement with a number of different clients afforded them an impressive pool of expertise and capability superior to most buyers to achieve cost and efficiency savings;

2   at that time the cost of mainframe data centre technology was falling as the market matured and more efficient and cost-effective computers became available;

3   data centres had very high fixed costs which included the mainframe itself, floor space and special cooling and power supply systems. Consolidating several data centres onto one site created considerable cost and resource savings;

4   the cost of telecommunications was falling – especially in the US – and telecommunications technology was developing so that geographic proximity of data centres to their users became less and less of an issue;

5   suppliers could use their size and hence buying power to leverage more cost-effective licence, lease and purchase contracts with third-party software and hardware vendors;

6   suppliers had considerably more immunity from internal buyer political pressure than the buyer's in-house functions, giving them the ability to implement cost reductions dispassionately across the outsourced function.

Organisations could not afford to ignore the opportunity to inject some certainty into their IT budgets and regain some control over this mysterious function. The outsourcing business began to grow rapidly and the various efficiency savings – some of which were passed on to the buyers – made this a very lucrative business for the rapidly increasing number of suppliers. It should be noted that large as these outsourcing deals were, they were very much restricted to organisations' IT operations rather than the more strategic elements of IT such as planning and development – which were generally regarded as too risky to place with a third party.

Outsourcing became a serious threat to IT managers who stood to lose considerable control and influence in their organisations. Their response was often to conduct their own cost reduction programmes and demonstrate their efficacy to senior management – sometimes through the medium of external benchmarking experts and consultants. IT departments took advantage of the efficiency savings that the outsource suppliers gave to their clients through consolidating data centres, acquiring newly available more efficient mainframe computers, increasing the level of data centre automation and relocating operations to more cost-effective sites. In terms of efficiency and effectiveness data centres were maturing swiftly, leaving less room than before for suppliers to make improvements and profits as large as they had previously done.

The buyers' attitude to outsourcing was also maturing. They swapped war stories, gathered 'best-practice' information, attended outsourcing conferences and hired lawyers and consultants with outsourcing expertise. Buyers demanded more services from their suppliers and as IT became more and more complex, they demanded greater acceptance of operational risk by suppliers.

The supplier market grew and so did the variety of service offerings. Suppliers broadened their IT outsourcing offerings to include, for example, the management of networks and personal computers. Non-IT services were included, such as the finance function, pensions administration, taxation and accounting services. Suppliers bolstered their expertise in functions like IT and finance with knowledge of their clients' markets. Suppliers also specialised in specific areas, a need partially forced upon them by the entry of other specialist suppliers into the outsourcing market and the increased complexity of the outsourced functions which they managed.

Suppliers also offered to take a greater share of their buyer's operational risks – and rewards. This willingness to accept more risk has extended the list of potential functions and processes which the buyer could outsource and the type of deal which it could structure with its supplier. If one imagines a line where simple FM contracts might occupy the leftmost point and, as one moves farther to the right, the type of outsourcing deal becomes more complex to operate and manage, the various risks to both parties of the deal failing increase but the cost and potential reward for both supplier and buyer also increase (*see* Figure 1.1). The position of an outsourcing deal on this continuum might be influenced by the:

- rate at which that function or process must change to ensure it provides its business users with the functionality they expect and;
- potential of that function or process to affect the buyer organisation's performance;

- degree of responsibility taken by the supplier for that function or process;

- contribution of that function or process to the buyer's revenue and profit stream.

Examples of types of deal along this continuum are given in Figure 1.1.

Figure 1.1
Deal characteristics

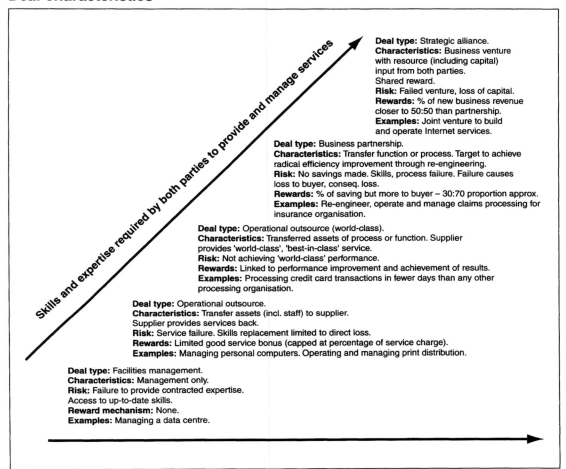

It is important to remember that, even though outsourcing has moved on in terms of the types of outsourcing opportunities available to organisations, this does not suggest that the older FM and operational outsourcing deals, with more limited risk exposure to the supplier, are being replaced by newer types of deal where the risks to the supplier are higher. Each of these types of deal solves a specific business issue and therefore all types are still in use today. The challenge for organisations is to select the most appropriate type of outsourcing deal for its particular business issue.

Benefits of outsourcing

A recent survey[2] of over 120 UK public and private sector organisations which have outsourced their IT functions cited the following reasons for outsourcing, ranked in order of popularity:

1 supplier is more cost effective than the in-house department;

2 greater supplier experience and expertise;

3 reduction of IT costs by supplier;

4 enables the buyer to focus on core business;

5 buyer resource constraints;

6 supplier provides access to new technologies;

7 lack of in-house skills;

8 flexibility for the future;

9 improved customer service quality.

An additional reason for outsourcing sometimes cited by senior managers is the enhancement of their financial and operational control of a particular function. Ironically an in-house function might be easier to control when outsourced as outsourcing often provides buyers with greater cost visibility of specific functions or processes, contractual controls and, as already mentioned, suppliers can often implement changes at their client's request more promptly and dispassionately than in-house management.

As well as the financial benefits of outsourcing, an increasingly important argument for outsourcing centres on skills retention. Particularly in the IT arena, where many countries are experiencing a shortage of IT skills, organisations are looking to third parties to take on the risk of sourcing and retaining IT skills and of controlling the relative cost of skills. In countries like South Africa, where last year the wage inflation of IT professionals was estimated to be in the region of 30 per cent, the outsourcing question was on the agenda for many organisations. Some suppliers were in a position to provide the services from other countries where the cost of skills was lower.

---

2   *The Maturing of Outsourcing* (London: KPMG, 1997).

Potential risks in outsourcing

Outsourcing can and does go wrong for many reasons. The worst-case scenario is litigation, disrupted services and a collapsed supplier relationship – although such a drastic conclusion to an outsourcing deal is unusual. However, even if an outsourcing deal rolls on year after year and the buyer fails to realise the expected benefits, then the deal must be deemed a failure. Unfortunately these situations are not as uncommon as they should be.

Some of the risks in outsourcing of which organisations must be aware are:

1 becoming locked into a supplier at a time when the organisation requires maximum flexibility;

2 outsourcing to a supplier which is subsequently acquired by a competitor of the buyer;

3 supplier insolvency;

4 the buyer organisation changing its corporate strategy in such a way that the outsourcing deal is no longer appropriate (*see* Chapter 4);

5 supplier failing to provide the contracted services to the required level;

6 buyer failing to include detailed service requirements in its contract with the supplier and incurring high charges for additional services.

The aforementioned survey cites the most popular reasons buyers are dissatisfied with outsourcing. These include:

1 over-dependence on the supplier;

2 becoming locked into the supplier and lacking flexibility;

3 lack of influence on the service levels of the supplier;

4 length of time for supplier to get the service right;

5 limited or no control over the supplier.

And finally, suppliers too have problems with their buyers. In no particular order, the following are frequently cited issues in relation to buyers:

1 too vague about requirements;

2 lack of clarity on what they are really outsourcing;

3 unrealistic expectations: expecting wonders – immediately;

4 little or no real in-house service measures, but expecting them from day one after the outsourcing contract;

5   allocating too few resources to the outsourcing process and contract management;

6   no attempt to set business expectations;

7   failing to inform staff of what's going on;

8   assuming it is all over once the deal is signed;

9   trying to solve a tactical issue with a strategic tool.

Functions which can be outsourced

A frequently asked question is: what can and cannot be outsourced? The simple answer is that practically everything can be outsourced, from part of a finance function (such as payroll processing or accounts receivable) to an entire function such as IT (*see* Figure 1.2). More recently, whole business processes such as large parts of back-office operations in financial services organisations have been targeted for outsourcing, along with the supporting finance, IT and human resources components of these processes. If both supplier and buyer can benefit then they will outsource – there are no boundaries. On the assumption that nothing is sacred, organisations are having to examine more carefully than ever the strategic implications of which parts of their businesses they retain and which parts they outsource. This discussion is expanded in Chapter 3.

Figure 1.2
Some functions typically outsourced

- IT operations and maintenance
- Development of applications
- PC support
- Payroll processing
- Human resources recruitment and expatriate management
- Tax management
- Accounts payable/receivable
- Call centres
- Help desks
- Manufacturing
- Procurement processes

Despite the broad potential scope of outsourcing, it is useful to consider the characteristics of those functions or processes that organisations have outsourced to date. Often the functions or processes most susceptible to outsourcing are those:

- which are essential to the organisation (high cost of failure) but with which the organisation has limited experience;

- where the organisation has traditionally had some difficulty, financial or other, managing that function or process;

- at which the organisation does not regard itself as an expert.

Additionally, organisations are usually more willing to outsource a function or process which is not regarded as one which differentiates them from their competitors but one which they nevertheless must perform as well as, if not better than, their competitors. Naturally the propensity to outsource is also a function of the capability and availability of suitable suppliers and the experience of other buyer organisations in general in this type of outsourcing.

Current outsourcing trends

The outsourcing market has grown rapidly and is estimated by some to be worth over $200 bn world-wide in transaction values per annum. Despite this growth, outsourcing has, until recently, focused very much on business support functions such as operational IT (including computer procurement, maintenance and operation), human resources and finance. Operating at this level, outsource suppliers are expected to focus on increasing functional efficiency and effectiveness.

More recently, suppliers have developed their business relationships with their clients beyond that of custodian of business functions to a more strategic position in their clients' organisations. As part of this more strategic role suppliers are taking on more of their clients' business risks. In return, where successful, they expect a share of the rewards. Such relationships are loosely referred to as 'partnerships',[3] 'strategic partnerships' or 'strategic alliances'. A typical deal of this kind might be the outsourcing of a number of business processes, such as logistics, to a supplier which will bear the cost of re-engineering these processes and will only profit if savings above a certain level are made or if the buyer's income is positively and quantifiably affected.

---

3.   It should be noted that this does not refer to a legal partnership between buyer and supplier.

Summary

Outsourcing is here to stay. As it continues to develop it will present new opportunities (and of course corresponding risks) for organisations. Businesses can steal a march on their competitors by utilising this very effective tool. Decision makers need to examine their portfolio of functions and processes, examine the outsourcing market's capability and question whether their organisations are at risk by *not* outsourcing. Finally, decision makers must understand what type of outsourcing deal they require, what the potential risks and benefits are and ensure they understand the risks that they are rewarding their suppliers for accepting and managing.

2

Understand the outsourcing process

Introduction

Outsourcing as a process is quite simple, but implementation can be extremely complex. Figure 2.1 shows the key elements of the process and identifies the tasks to be completed at each stage.

Figure 2.1
The outsourcing process

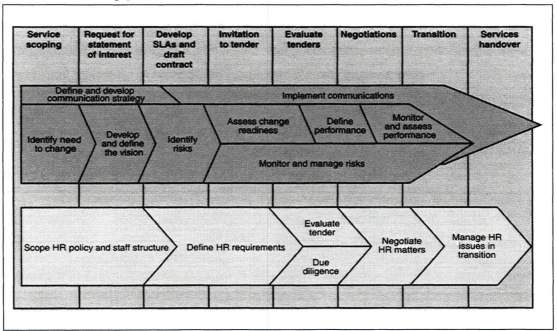

For simplicity the process is described below as a five-phase approach. The five phases of a typical outsourcing deal lifecycle are:

1   decide whether to outsource and clarify the scope of the deal;

2   select a supplier;

3   negotiate and sign a contract with the chosen supplier;

4   transfer the outsourced function to the supplier and manage the contract;

5   on termination decide whether to renew, retrieve or transfer to a new supplier.

This chapter gives an overview of these phases and points to some of the problems which may be encountered at each stage. Each phase is then dealt with in more detail in later chapters of the book.

The phases

Phase 1

Typically the decision to outsource is taken by the head of the function or process to be outsourced and ratified by the board or other senior management. For example, it would usually be an IT director's decision to outsource desktop personal computer services. However, where a business process such as claims administration in an insurance organisation is outsourced, along with the IT, HR, finance and other constituent components, a more integrated approach is required. The decision to outsource is critical to the organisation. It is dealt with in detail in Chapter 4.

WARNING

Various phases are sometimes cut short by the buyer and/or supplier in an effort to expedite the time taken to get to contract signature. This is a high-risk strategy which is discussed in Chapters 3 and 4.

Phase 2

Traditionally an organisation seeking a supplier issues a request for information (RFI) to a number of potential suppliers. Often an organisation will receive over ten 'statements of interest' from potential suppliers. In one case over 120 replies were received. However, this is more likely to testify to the vagueness of the RFI than the number of appropriate suppliers in that market. Usually this group is reduced to a smaller number of suppliers, typically between three and ten, to whom the organisation will issue a detailed invitation to tender (ITT).

Some suppliers may decide at this stage not to respond to (or to 'no bid') the ITT. It has been known for *all* suppliers to 'no bid' the ITT, although this is very rare. Suppliers which are preparing bids will usually expect to have a number of meetings with their potential client to further their understanding of the organisation and its requirements and to establish a relationship with key individuals. The returned bids are then assessed against a number of criteria which the buyer has developed (described in Chapter 5).

The list of potential suppliers is then reduced to one or two. It is often recommended at this point to keep at least two suppliers in the process in order to enhance the buyer's negotiation position. However, this can irritate suppliers and can be too confusing and resource demanding for the buyer to sustain. Following supplier presentations to the buyer's board or senior management a decision is made whether to go forward to the contracting stage or not – and with whom.

At this point a heads of agreement (or memorandum of understanding or letter of intent) is sometimes signed with the chosen supplier which sets out, among other things, the date by which the parties intend to sign the full agreement, the apportionment of costs if agreement is not reached and an outline of the key aspects of the deal.

Phase 3

The next phase is the drafting and negotiation of the main outsourcing agreement. This will typically comprise a number of operative provisions plus a number of schedules (described in Chapter 6). The most important schedule is the service level agreement (SLA) which is described in detail in Chapter 8. The SLA describes all of the services which the supplier will provide to the buyer as part of this agreement. One should assume that (subject to the precise wording of the agreement) if a service is not defined in the SLA, the buyer is not entitled to it.

Phase 4

A plan to implement the transition of the function or process from the client to the supplier should be compiled, agreed by both parties and included as one of the schedules to the agreement. A detailed transition plan is critical to reduce the risk of service disruption at the transfer date.

Throughout the life of the contract both parties will need to manage the services and the overall deal. Service management requires regular assessment of requirements and performance *by both parties*. Overall deal assessment should be performed against performance indicators, examples of which are provided in Chapter 9.

Phase 5

At the end of the contract the supplier and buyer will make a decision as to whether they will renew the contract. If the contract is not to be renewed, the client will also need to decide whether it wants to reclaim the services, transfer them to another supplier or fragment the outsourced function and deal with the different elements in different ways.

Summary

Different issues assume greater significance at different stages of the outsourcing process. In the initial stages, up to the signing of the contract, it is critical for the buyer to ensure it gets the best deal with the best supplier. After contract signing, the long process – for the life of the deal – of managing the contract with the supplier begins. This is a difficult process of which many buyers have not had prior experience. Buyers are often surprised at the amount of time and resource which are needed to fulfil this management task. Finally, at the end of the contract life, the buyer will need to decide the future of its outsourced function or process. This transition process can easily take six months or more, depending on the option chosen.

3

Put an effective outsourcing team in place

Introduction

For a buyer, a dedicated outsourcing team is essential to the success of an outsourcing project. It is important to note that this is the case not just at the time of contract signature, but also until the end of the outsourcing contract. Failure to put in place a dedicated team which is knowledgeable and experienced in the outsourcing process exposes the buyer organisation to the risk of not attaining the benefits expected from the outsourcing project. At best this will mean five to ten years of failed objectives; at worst it will result in financial loss and lack of organisational control and flexibility – handcuffing the buyer for the life of the contract.

This chapter sets out some guiding principles for good outsourcing teams, identifies the various areas of specialisation and indicates the skills sets which should be included in any outsourcing team.

Team objective

The objective of the outsourcing team must be to formulate and implement an outsourcing deal which delivers to the buyer organisation the anticipated benefits. This means not only finding a supplier that can deliver the benefits expected by the buyer organisation but also managing the deal with the supplier for the life of the contract. It is frequently the case that organisations use one team to find the supplier and close the contract and another team to manage the contract from the date of signature. The former team's objective (to find a supplier and close a contract) is likely to detract from the real objective of securing a deal which focuses on delivering benefits throughout the life of the deal. Additionally, deals done in this way can lack critical upfront thinking and fail to consider the various scenarios (such as acquisitions) which might occur during the life of the outsourcing contract. Finally, a team which will wash its hands of an outsourcing deal after contract signature is less likely to put effort into securing strong terms which will protect the buyer at the end of the contract life.

The stated objective therefore requires that, from the start, the team has a very clear understanding of the organisation's requirements and the expected benefits from the outsourcing deal. This issue is dealt with in more detail in Chapter 4. At this stage, suffice it to say that considerable initial effort must be invested to get a clear understanding of what benefits an outsourcing deal can deliver and how these match the organisation's requirements.

Important principles

Consistency must be the watchword for the outsourcing team, consistency in terms of its approach to the outsourcing process and in its dealings with suppliers and the rest of the buyer organisation. Consistency in its own composition is also important. The team will alter in composition as different skills are required at different times, but a core group should always remain in place to ensure knowledge retention and to provide a familiar face for suppliers and buyer user groups. Change to the core team is disruptive at any point in the lifecycle of the deal and particularly during the supplier selection and negotiation process prior to contract signature.

Team sponsorship is an essential ingredient of the success of the outsourcing deal and the team. The team will report to the person who, in the buyer organisation, is accountable for delivering to the organisation the outsourcing benefits. This is often the finance, information technology, operations or human resource director. This person (often referred to as 'the sponsor') is the ultimate decision maker throughout the outsourcing lifecycle and will rely heavily on the outsourcing team. The sponsor must ensure that, within the buyer organisation, the team is free to carry out its work and that it receives the necessary support from other directors and senior managers. The team's involvement with its sponsor will vary in intensity throughout the outsourcing lifecycle. Initially the team will work closely with the sponsor when defining the scope of the potential deal. Later on, during supplier evaluation, contract negotiation and signing, considerable sponsor involvement can again be expected. Once a firm contract is in place, sponsor involvement should generally be reduced to regular update meetings.

It is recommended in this book that organisations which rely on a considerable volume of outsourced services should appoint a senior figure to co-ordinate outsourcing across the organisation. For each specific outsourcing project that person should be a key adviser to the sponsor and to the outsourcing team. The role and objectives of this figure are described in more detail in the next chapter.

Finally, it is often the case that the quality of outsourcing deals suffers as a result of the availability – or lack of availability – of core team members. Today there are few organisations that are not resource constrained, but the importance of the outsourcing deal and the huge consequences of failure for the organisation should leave sponsors in no doubt that a dedicated outsourcing team is one of its highest priorities.

Team composition

The composition of the outsourcing team will change throughout the outsourcing lifecycle to accommodate different functional requirements. For example, the contracting stage of a deal requires considerable legal resource, but much less legal resource is usually needed once the contract is signed.

An effective way to tackle an outsourcing project is to split the outsourcing team into work streams. Each stream focuses on an area of activity which is critical to the success of the project and appropriate skills are recruited to each stream. Typical examples are shown in Table 3.1.

Table 3.1
Typical outsourcing team composition

Stream	Sample tasks	Typical expertise, skills and experience
Legal	Reflecting commercial principles in draft contract, contract negotiation with supplier, novation of licences to supplier	Legal – specifically in outsourcing, employment legislation, experience of contract novation
Finance	Financial modelling through the deal, understanding cost implications of options proposed by suppliers, identifying savings, e.g. asset disposal, tax	Accountancy, financial reporting and management
Asset	Decide which assets will be transferred, their value, whether they are leased or owned	Accountancy, audit
Commercial	Deal pricing mechanism, transfer values, compensation schemes, financing options	Finance, contract management, procurement, knowledge of the buyer's business requirements and objectives
Human resources	Identifying transferring staff, compliance with legal requirements, staff communication	Human resources, communications
Project	Overall project management and project office	Project management, communications, risk management
Service	Understanding service needs of the businesses, setting up service level agreements, assessing supplier service capability, monitoring service performance	Service management experience, previous SLA design, good knowledge of the function being outsourced

At least some, and ideally all, team members should have outsourcing experience. As organisations frequently do not have outsourcing expertise, some of the streams identified in Table 3.1 are likely to be staffed by external consultants and lawyers.

Team skills

Apart from the specific skills described in Table 3.1, there are a number of general skills and knowledge requirements which would benefit the outsourcing team. These include knowledge of project management and project planning plus presentation skills, facilitation skills, and negotiation and communications skills, the last being particularly important for those involved with the human resources aspects of the deal.

Risk management

Critical to the success of the entire outsourcing deal (and the thrust of this book) is the assurance that the outsourcing team is managing risk in a structured way. The team must be capable of identifying and predicting risks, developing solutions to deal with those risks and then implementing the proposed solutions. Maintenance of a risk register, regular team reviews of the register and frequent reporting to the sponsor of all risk reduction activities are all essential to the management of risk.

Summary

The outsourcing team is critical to the success of the outsourcing deal. It should be put in place when the buyer is considering outsourcing and should remain in place at least until the end of the outsourcing deal. The team must have clear objectives and a consistent approach to the project. It is often useful on complex projects to divide the team into work streams. The identification and management of risks must be a key focus of this team. The characteristics of a good outsourcing team are summarised in Figure 3.1.

Figure 3.1
Characteristics of a good outsourcing team

A good outsourcing team:

- understands the overall process;

- has one member to manage risks – usually the project manager;

- divides the process into several streams (legal, HR, service, commercial);

- has experts in each stream (who can operate in parallel);

- is dedicated to the task at hand;

- remains in place when the deal is signed to help manage the service.

Ten questions for the team

1   What is the team structure?

2   What are the team's skills and expertise?

3   What is the team's experience of outsourcing?

4   How is it planned to develop the team and cater for changing skills requirements at different phases?

5   What are the team's reporting and briefing processes?

6   Does the team understand the objectives of the deal?

7   Does the team already have a project plan?

8   Who does the team report to?

9   Which team members are dedicated to this project?

10 What would the team regard as failure?

4

Evaluate the case for outsourcing

Introduction

Whether to outsource or not is one of the most important decisions which any corporate decision maker will take on behalf of his or her organisation. It is a decision to be a specialist or to hire a specialist; to operate and manage or purely to manage; to make or buy; to relinquish control (and accept the consequences) or to retain control and forego potential outsourcing benefits. It is vital that the correct decision is taken as outsourcing is expensive and difficult to implement properly and is usually hard to reverse.

Before deciding whether to outsource, decision makers must be aware of the risks of outsourcing and of not outsourcing. They need to understand the goals and strategy of their organisation and the capabilities of the outsourcing market.

This chapter sets out some recommendations to senior executives who may be faced with having to decide whether to outsource or not. The recommendations are intended to reduce the organisation's risk exposure to outsourcing. Some of the risks described in this chapter are dealt with in greater detail elsewhere in this book, but this chapter asks decision makers to stop and think about outsourcing before going down that particular road.

Outsourcing – a subjective decision

The decision to outsource would be considerably easier to make if it were possible to run through an objective series of questions and come to a definitive yes or no answer. Sadly it is not that simple. Sometimes the deciding factor will be organisational policy, which can be nebulous and unwritten, rather than any hard financial requirements. To highlight the difficulty which may be faced, consider the following real-life example.

The Food and Drug Administration (FDA) requires clinical trial data to be retained for all drugs which are sold by pharmaceutical companies in the US. The data must be accessible to the FDA on request and must be accurate in order to allow the FDA to investigate any concerns with regard to a drug or its side effects. Failure to satisfy FDA requirements can lead to the retraction of the offending product from the US market.

A pharmaceutical company was recently deciding whether or not to outsource the storage and maintenance of its clinical trial data – both paper and electronic based. The argument for outsourcing was that it would be cheaper to outsource and would enable the buyer to take advantage of the potential supplier's expertise in data storage and protection. The potential supplier had better storage facilities than the pharmaceutical company and was more likely to succeed with a project to convert the paper-based data to a more accessible electronic form than the pharmaceutical company as its IT department was already implementing several other time-critical projects.

The counter-argument was that the clinical trial data were core to the organisation's existence, were highly confidential and should not be handed over to a third party. Another pharmaceutical organisation had a few months earlier considered a similar outsourcing of trial data and for this reason had chosen not to outsource.

The pharmaceutical company in question chose to outsource, subject to finding a suitable supplier and negotiating an acceptable contract. In support of the decision (and unlike its rival) this pharmaceutical company claimed that data storage and management was not one of its areas of specialisation. Managing a third party was, however, within its remit and as long as it did that correctly, it was irrelevant that the data were in the hands of a third party – in fact it was possibly advantageous as they might stand less of a risk of being destroyed.

It is often asked which of the two companies was right. The answer is that both may have been correct. One organisation took the decision that the data were critical and that it should be custodian of this critical resource. The other took the view that the data themselves were not critical, but rather the management of the data, and for this reason a specialist manager was the optimum solution. The important point is that each organisation understood the risks and benefits of each option. The pharmaceutical organisation which outsourced understood the risks of third-party involvement – highlighted below – and the pharmaceutical organisation which did not outsource was aware of the danger to its valuable resource if, like its competitor, it did not give the necessary attention to its critical data.

Have clear outsourcing objectives

Clarity is crucial to organisations that adopt the outsourcing solution: clarity of business objectives, clarity of supplier requirements and clarity of outsourcing process are all necessary to prevent subsequent buyer disillusionment.

Outsourcing is a tool for implementing corporate strategy. The performance of this tool must be measured across the organisation but effective performance indicators can only be applied when the objectives of the deal are clear. Buyers can then clarify what is required of their supplier, backed up by performance indicators or measures. Outsourcing can involve intense effort over a number of years, and without measures the focus of the deal is lost and lethargy sets in – on both sides.

As an example of the need for measures to be in line with the organisation's outsourcing objectives, consider a retail organisation seeking to expand its overseas operations. It plans to set up offices in some very remote locations in South East Asia and Africa but it requires these sites to have access to the company's existing information network. With several existing overseas sites it knows that it must become an expert at international data networking if it is to achieve this connectivity in a cost-effective way. It chooses to outsource the existing capability to a network service provider. The objective is clear: expand overseas operations. The supplier's performance measures are clear: manage the existing network to the required levels of service, provide connectivity to any location within the aforementioned region within a specific time period, and demonstrate a cost-effective network topology.

Once an organisation is clear on its outsourcing objectives it will seek a supplier which can deliver these objectives. It is rarely the case that the supplier will offer precisely what the buyer is looking for. This lack of an optimal fit – after an arduous search – sometimes causes buyers to accept the closest offer. Once again the risk is that the original objectives will not be met – albeit that this may only become apparent in two or three years' time. Buyers must be aware of the possibility that they may reach a point when they must accept that their objectives will not be met by the current options and resign themselves to looking further afield.

Finally, if outsourcing is critical for an organisation implementing its corporate strategy and subsequently that strategy changes, with the result that the outsourcing deal no longer 'fits' that strategy, the outsourcing deal may either have to be considerably reshaped or terminated. An example might be an organisation whose strategy is to optimise customer service and reduce cost by consolidating several functions into one or two locations and then managing these locations. It outsources the functions and a supplier manages the consolidation project. This consolidation is profitable for the supplier as it has agreed to reduce the cost of these processes to the buyer by 20 per cent per annum and is confident that it can achieve at least 30 per cent – the difference being pure profit. Three years later the buyer changes its strategy. It wants to address a customer focus issue by placing some of the consolidated core functions and processes geographically closer to its main customers. The result – partial deconsolidation of the processes and functions and a profitability issue for the supplier.

In some cases such a situation is impossible to predict; in others the full involvement of senior management in developing outsourcing objectives might unearth this scenario and allow the outsourcing team to include some contractual provisions to deal with it.

Beware of cost reductions as an objective

It is now an old outsourcing adage that outsourcing for cost reasons alone does not work. The reasoning behind this proposition is that:

- a typical outsourcing deal will change so much during its life that it is difficult to understand where the cost savings are. Buyers will take advantage of new functionality which the supplier offers and will pay more for it – making cost comparisons with the original in-house cost of provision difficult;

- outsourcing is in some cases a radical measure to achieve cost reductions. Before outsourcing, one needs to ask whether a team of external experts, hired for six months, could have delivered the required cost reductions. This may be a better option than handing over everything to a supplier for five to ten years to achieve the same objective;

- the cost reductions delivered by many outsourcing deals do not outweigh the cost to the organisation in terms of loss of control and flexibility.

Thus it is dangerous to focus too closely on cost reduction – what is required is a comparison of the 'value added' by the supplier and the commensurate charges.

Understand the risk–objective relationship

As discussed in Chapter 1, there are several types of outsourcing deal, ranging from a purely functional outsourcing (in which the supplier is paid to deliver a distinct output) to a partnership or strategic alliance (where the supplier is working closely with the buyer to provide a service where the risks and rewards of successful delivery are shared). Examples range from a simple service to print and distribute an organisation's customer invoices to the reorganisation of front-office services to increase buyer customer focus. Both types of deal have different risk profiles. The buyer must ensure that it understands where its outsourcing objective lies on this risk continuum and what risks it is exposed to at any point.

Be precise about the scope

Clear objectives must be bounded by a precise understanding of the intended scope of outsourcing within the organisation. The scope of outsourcing must be addressed at three levels:

1   the scope of the proposed outsourcing within the organisation – which functions or processes could be outsourced;

2   the potential boundary between buyer and supplier responsibility (at the level of the individual deal);

3   the potential for the scope of the buyer requirements to change over the life of the deal.

Scope of functions/services to be outsourced

Organisations should identify which functions and processes are candidates for outsourcing and which are not. This decision may change with variations in the organisation's strategy as well as with developments in the outsource supplier market. Identifying possible areas within the organisation for outsourcing and investigating market capability in these areas are essential components of the scoping exercise.

Supplier/buyer boundary

As clarity and consistency are essential ingredients of successful outsourcing deals, surprises can spell disaster. Unexpected additional service charges leave many buyers disillusioned with their outsourcing 'partner'. These 'additional charges' can represent a significant proportion of the annual service charge and can reduce the originally expected financial benefits of the deal. Buyers sometimes accuse suppliers of luring them into attractive deals and then, once the contract is signed, piling on additional charges to claw back the original benefits. These extra charges often result from misunderstandings between buyer and supplier over the boundaries or scope of their outsourcing deal. To reduce the risk of unwanted additional charges the buyer must:

•   Ensure there is no confusion over what services are to be provided. At a macro level, the simple test for this is to bring representatives of both organisations into a room and ask them each to confirm their understanding of the boundaries of responsibility in the deal. Mismatches often occur. At a micro level the detail of the division of responsibilities is (or should be) set out in the service level agreement (*see* Chapter 8).

- Be aware of the charging basis. Additional work performed by suppliers for their clients is extremely cost visible as suppliers will charge for every hour worked unless operating a fixed-price project. Buyers are sometime alarmed at the costs and claim that had they retained the outsourced function in house these projects would have cost considerably less. Possibly – but where the in-house function might bury a considerable amount of overtime the supplier will probably charge for all of it. Often the supplier simply makes the real costs more visible. Therefore organisations which are considering outsourcing should not outsource business areas that are likely to undergo significant change during the lifecycle of the deal unless the charges, a charging mechanism or, at the very least, a method of reaching a charging mechanism is agreed at the outset.

Often, had the buyer been more rigorous at the outset when defining the scope of the deal, there would be less room for confusion, dispute and disappointment at a later stage.

Changes over the life of the deal

Over the lifetime of a deal there will often be a number of one-off tasks for which the supplier will make an additional charge. These might include upgrades to ensure equipment is millennium compliant or tests of business continuity or disaster recovery plans. Wide-ranging alterations will occur if the buyer organisation merges with or acquires another organisation and the supplier is required to include these newly acquired functions or processes within the scope of the deal. While not every eventuality can be foreseen, the buyer should sit with the supplier at the outset of the deal to make an estimate – even a vague one – of the likely changes and how they might be dealt with both operationally and financially. This information should be fed into the relevant financial models.

Understand the trade-offs

Outsourcing involves a series of trade-offs which decision makers must understand. Those who do not understand this risk restricting their organisation's control over its own functions and processes and its flexibility to change them quickly. This section highlights some of those trade-offs and offers advice on reducing the trade-off risk when deciding whether to outsource or not.

Control

Outsourcing is often a trade-off between the loss of control of a function on the one hand and having access to the benefits of outsourcing on the other. A formerly in-house function which the buyer controlled will, after outsourcing, probably be located off site and can only be manipulated to the extent set out in the outsourcing contract. It is inevitable that buyers will lose some operational control over an outsourced function and it is critical that buyers ensure that the limited control which they retain is documented in the outsourcing contract. Careful consideration of operational requirements at the outset of the contract can help build some control into it.

Two other issues are interwoven with the issue of control:

- *Competitive suppliers.* It is a legitimate concern for buyers that their supplier might enter the buyer business market as a competitor, or that their supplier may be acquired by a competitor. The buyer should insist that this is a ground for terminating the outsourcing contract with the supplier. Additionally, the buyer must protect the intellectual copyright.

- *Insolvency.* Every buyer of outsourced services is exposed to the risk of their supplier becoming insolvent. To date this has been rare, but supplier collapses have occurred. Even where the supplier is eventually rescued by a management buyout or a 'white knight', the buyer may have concerns about the new management and/or future stability of their supplier. Buyers often attempt to mitigate the risk by regularly reviewing the supplier's financial statements and by scheduling frequent high-level meetings with the supplier to discuss the latter's financial performance. As part of this assessment buyers might consider requiring the supplier to divulge information on:

  - its annual revenue broken down by the number of current clients – particularly whether a substantial share of its revenue stream is derived from one client;

  - its client contracts, how many are due for renewal in the next two years and, where there is a large revenue dependency on one client, when that renewal is due;

  - the number of contract terminations in a year and the revenue impact.

To minimise the risks associated with the transfer of control, buyers should also ensure that audit rights are contractually secured. In addition, for businesses in the financial services sector there are specific requirements with regard to control and audit. As a starting point it is therefore necessary to consider the provisions of the Banking Act 1987 and the subsequent consultative paper prepared by the Bank of England and the Financial Services Authority.

Flexibility

Suppliers are often incentivised to reduce cost and increase efficiency. This is often done with military-style discipline, with the introduction of inflexibility into the outsourced function and restriction of the buyer's scope for making variations to the service. A simple but frequently quoted example is that of 'out-of-hours service'. Before outsourcing, a buyer could call its employees on a Friday and ask them to work at the weekend. Now, in the outsourcing deal, the buyer must check the contract, make a request to the supplier – which may possibly incur an extra charge – or even be rejected.

Skills

Outsourcing represents a massive skills drain from an organisation. The trade-off is the transfer of the risk of skills maintenance and replenishment to the supplier. Moreover, the buyer gains access to additional skills and expertise.

Information

There are risks associated with allowing a third party to have access to a buyer's confidential information, but the trade-off for the buyer is the potential access to the skills, methodologies and market knowledge of its supplier.

Profit

The newer 'strategic alliance' type of outsourcing deal, where risks and rewards are expected to be shared, is a trade-off between sharing with the supplier the buyer's profit (increased through some joint activity with the supplier) and making less profit but not having to share it with the supplier. The treatment of losses tends to mirror the treatment of profits. This is a gamble for the buyer but upfront financial modelling and scenario planning should quickly determine the viability of a venture.

Restricted choice

A situation can arise where an organisation feels it has no choice but to outsource. Suppliers wishing to break into a particular market such as call centre outsourcing or a specific sector such as financial services are often willing to make very attractive offers to potential clients, including upfront cash inducements and over-book-value payment for assets. These offers can blind the relative objectivity of the decision maker. Faced with such an offer, buyers are often tempted to skip the competitive tendering process –

usually actively encouraged by the supplier. While the benefits of this approach can be considerable, so too is the risk of failure. Buyers must place additional emphasis on understanding the potential risks of the deal and making provision for these in the outsourcing. In addition, putting inducements to one side, the buyer must ensure that it is satisfied with the supplier's capability to provide the proposed services or achieve the suggested targets set out in the contract and specifically the SLA.

Multiple suppliers

Many of the risks discussed in this section stem from the dependence of the buyer on the supplier. Some buyers have hedged this dependence risk by dividing up large outsourcing deals into several pieces and outsourcing these to different suppliers – putting their eggs in more than one basket. In fact, some organisations sometimes preclude existing suppliers from tendering for new work. The trade-off in this scenario is that, while there is a degree of risk-spreading, a new risk is introduced. This is the management of multiple suppliers and the often cited problem of suppliers passing responsibility between each other – with the buyer the only loser. Greater attention is required to scope overlapping multiple supplier deals. Buyers have tended to spurn the advice to avoid multiple supplier outsourcings, tending instead to accept the risk in return for having several specialist suppliers rather than one generalist. This has been particularly evident in IT, where buyers often use different suppliers to provide data centre, personal computer, call centre, and print and distribution services.

Develop an outsourcing competency

Organisations now depend on outsourced services more than ever before. This dependence must be expected to increase in the future, along with the tendency for organisations to use several suppliers in parallel. A recent survey[1] carried out by KPMG found that more than 70 per cent of the 120 organisations polled used more than one supplier for the provision of IT services, with some having deals with up to 11 suppliers. Organisations will need to develop competencies at two levels to minimise this dependency on outsourced services.

First, at a high level, they must maintain a corporate overview of the role that outsourcing plays in delivering the organisation's strategy. This can be done in the following way:

---

1. *The Maturing Outsourcing* (London: KPMG, 1997).

1 A position should be created in the buyer's organisation with responsibility for outsourcing throughout the organisation. The holder must be charged with:

- co-ordinating outsourcing throughout the organisation;

- aligning outsourcing with the organisation's goals and objectives;

- ensuring existing deals perform as expected;

- resolving high-level issues on specific deals;

- co-ordinating learning across several outsourcing deals;

- ensuring consistency of approach when procuring outsource suppliers;

- keeping abreast of the outsourcing market and what it can offer the organisation;

- understanding and implementing best-practice, proactive service management;

- playing an internal consulting role in specific outsourcing deals, supporting and advising the outsourcing team where necessary.

The holder of the position should report to a board member and preferably, to ensure consistency and convenience, to the sponsor who will sign off each outsourcing deal on behalf of the organisation.

2 An outsourcing strategy should be created and maintained. The outsourcing strategy should set out clearly: the competencies which the organisation wishes to retain in house and those which are potential targets for outsourcing; the objectives of outsourcing and possible performance indicators which are consistent with the organisation's strategic objectives; strategies for monitoring existing and past outsourcing deals; and the risks to the organisation posed by outsourcing generally and by the specific risks of each outsourcing deal. The objective of this outsourcing strategy is to:

- achieve focus for outsourcing within the organisation and particularly at a senior management level;

- place outsourcing as a key part of annual strategic planning;

- help consolidate learning on outsourcing;

- force active monitoring of competitors, suppliers and the outsourcing market;

- help monitor the risk profile of all outsourcing deals at a senior management level.

The outsourcing strategy should be reviewed regularly by senior management.

The second level of competency required is in the management of specific outsourcing deals. In this book 'contract management' includes:

- relationship management;

- service management;

- change management;

- performance management.

The above contract management competencies are described in Chapter 9.

Summary

In business terms the turn of the twentieth century must surely be remembered as the era of specialisation. Strategists are challenging organisations to choose their specialist activities and shed the rest. The days of the generalist are numbered. Organisations have responded with vigour, transacting unprecedented numbers of acquisitions, mergers, demergers and reorganisations. These organisations surround their remaining specialist activities or competencies with support functions and processes whose effectiveness and efficiency are critical to the value of the business.

The drive to improve the performance and reduce the cost of the support functions and processes has led organisations to look to third parties for help and has created an outsourcing business of immense scope and size. If an organisation is to achieve the full benefits of outsourcing it will need to develop an in-house contract management competency and ensure that outsourcing is represented at the highest level.

Ten questions for the team

1   Is the outsourcing deal consistent with corporate strategy?

2   What are the objectives of the deal?

3   What is the boundary of the outsourcing deal?

4   What additional costs are forecast for the life of the deal?

5   What are the key risks posed by this deal to the organisation?

6   How are these risks dealt with?

7   How will the deal be resourced?

8   Does a financial model exist for this deal?

9   What are the key components of your outsourcing strategy?

10   Who is your sponsor?

5

Select the best supplier

Introduction

Before seeking a supplier, the buyer will have already set its outsourcing objectives which will reflect the benefits it wants to achieve from outsourcing and the measures it will use to monitor whether these objectives are attained. With this clear view of its requirement, the buyer is ready to find and choose the supplier which can deliver these benefits.

Choosing a supplier which cannot deliver the anticipated outsourcing benefits can lock the buyer organisation into a relationship for several years that not only fails to deliver the advantages which justified the deal to the board in the first place, but also restricts the buyer's ability to achieve what it could have done without outsourcing.

Choosing the 'right' supplier is no final guarantee of a successful outsourcing deal, but getting the wrong one sets the risk of an unsuccessful deal at an unacceptable level.

This chapter makes four recommendations to buyers seeking a supplier. It begins by defining the 'right' supplier. It then helps the reader to compile a comprehensive list of potential outsourcing suppliers and goes through a process for specifying its outsourcing requirements. Finally, the issues and risks around the final selection procedure are described.

Define the 'right' supplier

The definition of the right supplier is different for each individual buyer. Fundamentally the supplier must be able to deliver the outsourcing benefits which the buyer expects. The supplier must satisfy a number of criteria in order to convince the buyer of its ability to do this. Broadly these criteria can be grouped into a number of different areas. The buyer must select the attributes in each area that would best match its requirement. The areas are as follows:

- *Expertise.* This includes the supplier's knowledge of specific industry sectors, specific functions or processes within those sectors and specific skills within those functions or processes. For example, a buyer's skills requirement might include insurance sector → claims handling process → IT programming skills in Java.

- *Capability.* This defines what the supplier is able to deliver as a result of experience of similar deals and the way in which it harnesses the expertise within its organisation. Capability requirements can differ considerably from buyer to buyer and can be quite complex. One buyer may seek a supplier with a capability to operate its payroll process in one UK city, while another may require a world-class or best-in-class capability in supply chain procurement in 27 countries. As many organisations drive to become 'global', such requirements are becoming more common and are presenting new challenges to suppliers.

- *Values.* Supplier values are very important to buyers. Values such as fairness, openness, professionalism and honesty are often tested by buyers during the outsourcing process. Buyers are often particularly concerned with suppliers' attitudes to buyer staff who will transfer to the supplier as part of the outsourcing deal, as they do not want their staff to be treated as second-class citizens (or, indeed, made redundant) by suppliers.

- *Control.* This covers the financial stability, structure and ownership of the supplier. In addition, a buyer should consider the implications of the supplier's existing client base. For example, would a buyer consider a supplier which already operates an outsourcing deal for a competitor?

Buyers must ensure that they have an understanding of what they are looking for in a supplier. The various attributes must not just satisfy their immediate requirements but also their expected needs for the life of the deal. With an understanding of these requirements the buyer is in a good position to approach the market and find a suitable supplier.

Compile a list of potential suppliers

Buyers need to ensure that when selecting a supplier they are choosing from the best possible pool of potential suppliers. They must reduce the risk of missing the best deal because the wrong suppliers were approached – or the right supplier was not approached. This is less of an issue for the public sector in Europe where public sector buyers are often required to use the *European Journal* to publish their requirements. This tends to leave the initiative with the supplier rather than the buyer seeking the supplier (which tends to be the norm in the private sector).

A buyer will want to understand which suppliers have the relevant expertise and capability. This information is often available from specific directories to which suppliers contribute. These directories, however, have certain limitations. They generally do not specify in which sectors different suppliers are strongest and they tend to be country specific, making it difficult to understand whether suppliers have truly international supply capabilities. However, this information can often be collated from press articles and trade journals.

Additional sources of information include the following:

- *The Internet.* Many suppliers now advertise their services on the Internet. This source is particularly good for finding suppliers with international capabilities.

- *Consultants and lawyers.* Many of the consultancies and law firms have advisory practices which specialise in outsourcing. These specialists will often have valuable experience or knowledge of the players in the market.

- *Specialist groups.* There are a number of groups which focus on developing current thinking on outsourcing (such as the Outsourcing Management Group). As the groups tend to work with both buyers and suppliers, their knowledge of the relevant markets is often very valuable.

At the end of this information gathering process, a buyer can usually expect to have in the region of ten organisations on its list of potential suppliers.

Specify outsourcing requirements to interested suppliers

The buyer will now issue a request for information (RFI) to the selected suppliers. The objective of the RFI is twofold:

1 to find out if a supplier is interested in bidding; and

2 to solicit more information from the supplier regarding the supplier's expertise and capability.

The RFI will typically be a letter or short document which contains:

- a brief description of the buyer's business, location and markets;

- an outline of the functions and/or processes to be outsourced;

- a statement of the expected benefits to be achieved from the outsourcing;

- a request for information about the supplier's expertise and capability and why it thinks it can satisfy the buyer's requirements.

The RFI will also include provisions dealing with a number of procedural issues, including:

- a statement that the buyer can choose to reject any supplier at any time;

- a request for a written response in a specified format within a given time period; and

- instructions on how the supplier should contact the buyer.

As the buyer is likely to want to limit the number of people (both within and outside its organisation) who are aware of the potential outsourcing, it should nominate only one central point of contact for suppliers and require the supplier to commit to binding confidentiality obligations. This approach reduces the likelihood of staff inadvertently discovering that they might be part of an outsourcing deal and also ensures a more level playing field for a competitive tendering process.

Two problems which might occur during this stage are as follows:

- The buyer already has a supplier for other outsourced services and must decide whether to send the RFI to that supplier. A buyer might choose to include the supplier because it has the necessary expertise and capabilities; it already has a relationship with the buyer; it understands the buyer organisation; and deal costs might be lower as the supplier may be able to offer a better price in the light of the expanded scope of its business with the buyer. Alternatively a buyer may deliberately exclude an existing supplier because of fear of organisational dependence on one supplier; to restrict the chance of other potential suppliers being deterred from tendering; and because of concerns that bidding could distract the supplier from its existing work within the organisation.

- None of the canvassed suppliers bid in response to the RFI. This occurs rarely but can happen if the suppliers regard the deal as too small to be worth the cost of tendering or too far away from their core business for them to be able to add much value to the buyer. Regardless of the reason, the buyer should contact the suppliers and find out their reasons for not replying.

However, assuming this last hurdle has been avoided, the buyer should now have a number of responses from suppliers interested in tendering. Ideally the list of potential suppliers will have been reduced to approximately three or four.

Once the buyer has a shortlist of potential suppliers it must prepare a document describing in detail its requirements. This document is generally referred to as an invitation to tender (ITT). Work on the ITT should have been progressing in parallel to the supplier selection procedure to avoid any unnecessary delays.

The buyer will have to invest considerable time in preparing the ITT. A good ITT should be:

- *easy* to understand for the supplier – does not use jargon specific to the buyer;

- *complete* in its description of what the buyer is looking for. Where an ITT is incomplete a considerable amount of time may be wasted later amending the supplier's bid. A supplier may even withdraw from the bidding as a result of last-minute 'surprises';

- *clear* in its description of the buyer's requirements. Vague statements often abound in ITTs and only serve to confuse suppliers;

- *precise* in specifying the process suppliers must follow to respond to the ITT.

The ITT usually comprises six main sections:

1 *Introduction.* This section includes the purpose and structure of the ITT, the buyer's reasons for outsourcing and its expectations from its future supplier.

2 *Instructions.* This section describes the tendering timetable and the overall outsourcing project timetable; sets out points of contact for ITT-related questions; specifies the number of references that the supplier is expected to provide and the number of copies of the bid required.

3 *Requirements.* This section sets out clearly and in detail the buyer's requirements. Clearly defined services in terms of their description and boundaries are specified (taking account of the buyer's commitments to its own customers), along with geographic coverage requirements and service performance needs. The buyer will also include a description of items which it considers to be beyond the scope of the deal, such as the control of policies and standards. Pricing requirements may also be dealt with – thus the buyer may stipulate that it wishes the bid price to be itemised by service and calculated as a quarterly charge.

4 *Transferring assets.* This section outlines the type, quantity and other details of the assets which the buyer will transfer to the supplier. Where a transfer of people will occur, information about the number of staff, their skills and expertise, is also supplied.

5 *Evaluation.* This section lists the different areas (similar to those described in 'Define the "right" supplier') against which the suppliers will be evaluated. Each area will need to be broken down further and for each section there should be one or more questions or statements of requirement for the supplier to respond to. For example, a sample question on personnel would be: 'Describe your staff training and development policy and how it will benefit the staff transferred under TUPE.'

> **NOTE:** In some cases buyers place many, many questions in this section which do not add much to the evaluation itself. Sometime this is because the questions came from a standard list obtained elsewhere. Having to answer each and every question is understandably irritating for a supplier. Buyers should assess the value of each question in determining the best supplier for their organisation.

6 *Contracting principles.* This section sets out the buyer's position on a number of key issues which should be agreed before going forward. Examples include an acknowledgement that both parties recognise that TUPE will apply to any staff transfer, that the supplier will give certain warranties and indemnities and that a specified limit on liability is agreed (*see* Figure 5.1). The advantage of the approach of including these points in the ITT is that fundamental differences of opinion, if they exist, are discovered at this point rather than later when the buyer's negotiating position is considerably weakened. This is a very important section of the ITT as a failure to agree on a point here could mean the rejection of the supplier's tender.

Figure 5.1
Contracting principles to be included in the ITT

- Warranties from the supplier that its equipment is millennium compliant
- Limits on liability
- Provisions re employee transfers
- Indemnities covering infringement of intellectual property rights
- Performance standards
- Responsibility for due diligence
- Responsibility for asset transfers

It is clear that the buyer will need to invest a considerable amount of time compiling the details described above. Much of this work will provide input to the schedules of the main contract, which is discussed in the next chapter. Where contracting principles are set out in the ITT, these should form the framework of the outsourcing contract.

Two additional issues need to borne in mind at this time:

- *Drafting control.* The buyer may stipulate that it will control the drafting of all documents, including the main contract and the schedules (including the SLAs). Suppliers often volunteer to take on this time-consuming task, an offer gladly accepted by buyers whose resources may already be overstretched. However, there are advantages for a buyer when it places its draft contract on the table for discussion. Much of what it wants should be in that draft and it is certainly easier to negotiate from such a position of strength than to negotiate new provisions into a supplier-favoured contract. While the overhead is high, the benefit of drafting control usually outweighs the cost.

- *Bidding process.* As buyers can become overwhelmed by the amount of information which they must compile, a supplier may offer to help the buyer cut the bidding process short by entering into a contract negotiation immediately – if the buyer rejects all other potential suppliers. Bidding is an expensive process for suppliers (costs can sometimes be in the region of £1 m), especially if they lose. However, as previously indicated, this approach increases the buyer's risk of not getting the best supplier.

Once the buyer sends out its ITT to potential suppliers it will need to be available to deal with suppliers' questions and requests for clarification. In parallel it will continue to develop SLAs (unless this is to be undertaken by the supplier later in the process), design a supplier evaluation matrix and create and implement a communications plan to inform staff of the deal and thereafter to keep them up to date on developments. As the deadline for supplier responses nears and the tender documents arrive at the buyer's office, the buyer's outsourcing team will prepare to choose its outsource supplier.

Choose the best supplier

Once the deadline for receipt of tender documents has passed, the buyer begins the formidable task of:

- ensuring that each response is complete and that where, for example, evaluation questions are not complete, the supplier is requested to fill in any missing information;
- confirming receipt of each supplier's response;
- evaluating each response document – making a note of issues to address with each supplier;
- inviting suppliers to make presentations on ITT-related topics;
- visiting reference sites provided by the supplier; and
- presenting findings to the project sponsor.

The buyer's outsourcing team should then create an evaluation matrix (*see* Figure 5.2). This lists each requirement to be evaluated, together with a weight indicating its importance to the buyer. A value representing the suitability of each supplier's response to each requirement is estimated by the outsourcing team and a total (value × weight) is calculated for each requirement. These are then added to give the supplier's overall total.

The attributes included in the evaluation matrix should reflect the questions asked in the evaluation section of the ITT and any additional attributes which the outsourcing team considers important. It should be noted that the evaluation matrix may contain over 100 attributes.

Figure 5.2
Sample evaluation matrix

Attributes (sample)	Weight (1–5)	Supplier outcome (1–5)	Total
Alignment with buyer strategy	5	2	10
Sector expertise	4	5	20
Benchmarking capability	3	4	12
Total Supplier A			42

Buyers should consider a threshold value for the result obtained from the evaluation matrix below which a supplier is disqualified. This is to ensure that, despite being the best-performing supplier to be evaluated, if the 'fit' with the buyer's requirements is not good enough, the supplier should automatically be disqualified.

Generally, as the evaluation matrix is compiled, one or two front runners will emerge from the list of potential suppliers. However, the others should not be written off too quickly, as it is sometimes the case that a supplier further down the field revises a key part of its bid in the light of additional discussions with the buyer and increases its total score in the matrix.

For additional leverage, some buyers recommend keeping two or more suppliers in the race throughout the contract negotiation process. While it might be useful to play one off against the other to secure better terms, it is not generally a feasible option for two reasons. First, suppliers will realise what is happening and may retract from the bidding. Second, the buyer usually cannot commit anything like the resource required to maintain several bidders in the race for the necessary length of time.

It is important to mention visits by the buyer to existing outsourcing clients of the supplier. Buyers often report at the end of the bidding process that these site visits contributed considerably to the final decision. Despite the fact that the supplier will choose carefully the best of its client sites to impress the buyer, the visits still tend to give the buyer a good indication of the type of supplier it is dealing with. The value of these visits cannot be overemphasised and a buyer should never enter into an outsourcing contract without visiting the site of at least one of the supplier's clients.

Frequently commitments are made by suppliers to a buyer during the various meetings, presentations and the exchange of correspondence in the tendering phase. These should be fully documented to avoid the danger that they are forgotten when the outsourcing contract is being prepared. The supplier will often insist that the contract include a statement that no reliance can be placed on pre-contractual representations, thereby reducing the value of any assurances given by the supplier during the tendering phase which are not included in the contract.

A large amount of the work described in this chapter is carried out by the buyer's outsourcing team. A recommended structure for this team is given in Chapter 3. The team must keep the key decision maker within the buyer organisation abreast of developments as the tendering process progresses, and finally feed back the results of its evaluation. Based on the team's presentation and usually following a presentation to the board, the successful supplier will be selected. At this stage it is important for the decision maker to meet and establish a relationship with senior management from the chosen supplier. This contact will be useful during the contract negotiation process for the reasons set out in Chapter 6.

Once the supplier selection has been made, the buyer may wish to secure an interim arrangement with that supplier. Often called a heads of agreement or memorandum of understanding, this document sets out, among other things, the date by which the parties intend to sign the full agreement, the apportionment of costs if agreement is not reached and an outline of the key aspects of the deal (often mirroring the contractual issues dealt with in the ITT), including the services that will be provided by the supplier, the number of people transferring, the costs, limits on liability and the duration of the deal.

Summary

Defining and finding the 'right' supplier is a difficult task requiring diligent work often over several months. Buyers must be very sure that the supplier, which will become an integral component of their business for the foreseeable future, is the best one available. The tendering process does have short cuts which carry associated risks. Buyers that take these risks may see the first sign of difficulties developing at the contracting stage.

6

Build a robust outsourcing contract

Introduction

The cornerstone of the relationship between buyer and supplier in an outsourcing deal is the contract. It reflects the agreed position on a range of commercial points such as the type of service that the supplier will provide, the scope of the service, the duration of the contract and the charging arrangements. The contract will determine the relative exposure of the buyer and seller to the various risks of the outsourcing deal, both in terms of what is included and what is excluded from the contractual terms.

It is critical for any buyer to ensure that the contract contains all of the commercial points required to secure the buyer's outsourcing requirements and that these points reflect an acceptable level of risk to the buyer. This chapter addresses these two critical issues. It begins at the point where the buyer plans its negotiation strategy and describes the preparation required to ensure all commercial points are included in the contact. The main sections of an outsourcing contract are then described, followed by a brief description of the negotiation process. Finally the need for a communications plan is explained.

Preparation

The objective of the negotiation process is to arrive at a signed contract which meets the needs of both parties. The first step is to prepare a draft contract. This is often an easier task for the supplier as it will probably have a standard form agreement. Buyers will not normally be so fortunate; if the legal stream of the outsourcing team has not been involved in an outsourcing project before it will probably not have a sample outsourcing contract to hand and may require external legal assistance. However, from the buyer's perspective there are disadvantages with using supplier standard form agreements (*see* drafting control in Chapter 5).

From the buyer's perspective the draft contract needs to take account of the following:

- technical requirements set out in the original ITT;
- legal requirements described in the contracting principles section of the ITT;
- expertise and capability statements included in the supplier's tender;
- additional requirements which the outsourcing project team identifies during the tendering stage;
- input from consultation sessions with transferring employees;

- supplier response to evaluation questions in the ITT;

- supplier correspondence with the buyer during the tendering stage;

- input from supplier site visits;

- presentations made by the supplier during the tendering stage.

The contract

An outsourcing contract usually involves both the transfer of assets from the buyer to the supplier and the acquisition of services by the buyer from the supplier. Each of these transactions can be described in the same contract or the two elements can be split into two contracts. In the interest of simplicity, this chapter assumes that both transactions are described in one contract.

A typical outsourcing contract comprises four main sections as follows:

- *Transfers.* This section deals with the assets that the supplier will take over, including hardware, software, contracts and personnel.

- *Service provision.* This section describes the services which the buyer will purchase from the supplier, the scope of the services and performance standards.

- *General legal provisions.* This section includes details of warranties, indemnities, liability, termination and pricing.

- *Exit arrangements.* This section describes the rights and liabilities of both parties at the end of the deal.

The main points addressed in each part of the contract are described in more detail in the following sections.

Transfers

This section deals with the transfer to the supplier of all 'in-scope' assets. The first step is to identify these assets, which are usually listed in the various schedules. Assets can include:

- buildings;

- office furniture;

- company cars;

- consumables (printing paper, blank forms);

- intellectual property (in relation to the transferred functions or processes, such as buyer-owned software, records and know-how, including processes and procedures);

- computer hardware (mainframe computers, personal computers, telecommunications equipment);

- licences in relation to third-party computer software;

- third-party supply agreements.

The contract will need to address the following issues.

Software licences

Who will approach the third-party licensors to obtain the necessary consents for the transfer (or other change to the licence terms)? The licensors often use this as an opportunity to require the payment of additional licence fees – which can be substantial. An unreasonable licensor can make demands which threaten the entire cost justification for the deal, so it is important that this issue is addressed at an early stage. The contract should also deal with the worst-case scenario – of the buyer not wishing to proceed as the consent cannot be obtained or only obtained at a prohibitive cost – by enabling the buyer to walk away at this stage.

Costs

Particularly in relation to hardware it is usual for the supplier to pay the buyer for the equipment transferred. The price is usually based on the asset's written-down book value or, sometimes less favourably for the buyer, market value.

Quality

The supplier may require warranties in relation to the performance of the transferred assets. The buyer would be advised to resist this, particularly if the supplier has carried out due diligence. If such warranties are not given, the supplier may require a reduction in its service performance commitments until it has had time to carry out any necessary upgrading or equipment replacement.

> **Due Diligence**
>
> **Due diligence** is the process of ascertaining the identity, quantity and quality of the assets to be transferred. It can also encompass the detailed definition of the services or functions to be outsourced.
>
> One of the key due diligence issues is timing. Buyers often insist that suppliers carry out due diligence *before* signing the contract. This can, however, take a considerable amount of time, which the parties may not have. The suppliers often want to delay due diligence until *after* signing the contract, which represents a bigger risk for the buyer.

Personnel

People are usually a key asset in an outsourcing transaction. Again the contract will need to identify those staff who will transfer (and a comprehensive list of names and job titles should be included in a schedule). The contract will then need to include the following:

- *State whether TUPE applies.* This is a complex area and specialist legal advice should be sought. Suffice to say that if TUPE does apply, the position is simplified as the contracts of employment automatically transfer. If not, the supplier is obliged to offer the employees employment on specified terms.

- *Include appropriate HR indemnities.* It is the usually accepted starting point that the buyer should retain the risk (and bear the cost) of all HR-related issues prior to the transfer date (including any outstanding claims in relation to sexual or racial discrimination, accrued holiday pay and bonuses), with the supplier giving a reciprocal indemnity for the period after the transfer.

- *Set out the procedure to be followed in relation to the consultation requirement imposed by TUPE.* These procedures are complicated if the buyer is unionised and it is advisable to involve the union representatives from an early stage.

- *Deal with the transfer of any pension entitlements.* Pensions are not covered by the automatic transfer provisions in TUPE and will therefore need to be dealt with separately. This is a complex area which is beyond the scope of this book. However, it is important to remember that, depending on the type of pension scheme involved, it may be necessary for the actuaries of the buyer and supplier to be involved. This takes time, and if an analysis of the respective pension funds shows there is an imbalance in terms or any under-funding, money may need to change hands. Again, such payments can be substantial and may change the financial attractiveness of the deal (for either party).

Transition

The contract should then deal with the physical transition of these in-scope assets to the supplier. Ideally the detailed arrangements should be set out in a transition plan. The contract should specify the following:

- Who will create the transition plan?
- How will the plan be tested?
- Who is liable if the transition fails?
- What is the fall-back position if it fails?

An interesting point to note is that a contract often stipulates that a supplier must begin service provision from its site at midnight on a particular date using equipment leased by the buyer. However, the lease of the equipment only transfers to the supplier at the cut-over time (i.e. midnight). If the equipment (often computer hardware) needs to be physically relocated, it must be moved before midnight – when it is still technically leased by the buyer. In the event that the supplier damages the equipment while transporting and/or installing it, then it should be liable for the repair of the equipment and service impact costs – despite the fact that the buyer is still the lessor at the time the damage occurs.

Service provision

This section of the contract describes the services which the buyer will receive from the supplier. The detailed service descriptions are usually set out in the SLA, which will be a schedule to the main contract. The following points will need to be addressed.

Service performance

The SLA will set out specific, quantitative performance obligations (as described in Chapter 8), but the contract should also contain general, qualitative performance standards such as an obligation to use all reasonable skill and care and to ensure all the personnel are properly trained, and, possibly, a commitment to deliver 'best-in-class' services.

Service delivery obligations

The continued provision of service is critical to the buyer. The contract should try to minimise any risks that the supplier could stop providing service for any reason, including failure of the buyer to pay a disputed invoice, other disputes between the parties and any service failures by its subcontractors.

Critical service staff

A well aired concern of buyers is that after the contract is signed their supplier may replace the team providing the service with a less effective team, resulting in service degradation. Buyers would therefore be advised to insist that certain individuals are dedicated to it and that all staff are of a certain calibre. Naturally, suppliers cannot prevent specified individuals from leaving their organisation, but they can ensure that they continue to be allocated to a buyer while still employed.

Change control

Throughout the life of the deal the supplier will need to make changes to the services. Some of the changes will be at the request of the buyer, others may be part of the supplier's own service improvement initiatives. The buyer will need to ensure that:

- changes are only made in accordance with the procedure set out in the contract and are all documented;

- the supplier is obliged to produce an impact assessment in relation to any proposed change at no additional cost to the buyer;

- all significant changes are first agreed with the buyer;

- it can veto changes which it believes will have a negative impact on its services now or in the future;

- the charging arrangements (at least in outline) for any changes to the services are specified.

Service benchmarking

Some buyers request that their supplier benchmark its capability against an industry standard. This is a useful way to demonstrate and test the quality of the service provided. Not everything can be benchmarked, but at least some elements of the service can usefully be compared with those provided by other suppliers. Benchmarking can be applied to costs, performance or both. There are a number of generally used cost benchmarks such as 'cost per payslip' for payroll services, 'cost per seat' for call centre services and 'annual cost per personal computer' for personal computer services. Particular care must be taken with the composition of these benchmarks so that a like-for-like comparison is made.

Service documentation

Documents such as procedures manuals can contain valuable know-how whose worth would become very apparent on termination. The supplier should therefore be required to provide such manuals and then regularly update and maintain them.

Service reporting

It is important for the buyer to monitor service performance and the supplier should be obliged to produce detailed, frequent reports to facilitate this.

Audit

The buyer needs to be able to verify that the supplier is charging in accordance with the agreed pricing arrangements and that performance standards are being adhered to. Both these rights are secured by appropriate audit provisions.

Disaster recovery

The division of responsibility between the buyer and supplier in the event of a 'disaster' (such as the destruction of or inability to use the premises from where the services are provided) needs to be clear. When a 'disaster' actually occurs there must be no possibility of confusion about who needs to do what.

Service infrastructure and innovation

The buyer is advised to retain a degree of control over the technology platform used by the supplier, at least in terms of interface compatibility with the buyer's platform. This is an ongoing issue – over time the supplier may need to make technology changes or re-engineer processes to fulfil a cost reduction commitment in the pricing framework. However, it should not be entitled to do this if it leads to the buyer incurring other costs or if it produces interface compatibility problems.

General legal provisions

Many of the fundamental principles around which the agreement is structured are described in this section. Failure to give special consideration to these points can expose the buyer to significant risks. Some of the key points are as follows.

Payment

Adopting the right charging mechanism for the services supplied is key to the success of any outsourcing (as discussed in detail in Chapter 7). The contract must document these charging arrangements – not just for continuing services, but also for future and special, one-off services (e.g. disaster recovery testing). In addition, payment dates, method, destination and frequency should be described as well as the mechanism for handling payment adjustments for poor or exceptional service (if applicable). Buyers are advised to insist on financial visibility in relation to the supplier's charging arrangements to minimise the risk of over-charging.

Indemnities

The buyer should consider seeking indemnities from its supplier:

- if the supplier infringes the intellectual property rights of a third party. The supplier must ensure that it is properly licensed to use the third-party software which it needs to provide the buyer's services. If it does not have the necessary licences or authorisation, the third party may bring an action for infringement of intellectual property rights. This should be a cost for the supplier and the buyer should be protected from any such claims;

- in respect of certain personnel issues (*see* the section on 'Transfers' earlier in this chapter);

- to cover any personal injury or property damage.

Warranties

The buyer might require warranties from the supplier that:

- the supplier will ensure that the facility from where the services are provided is secure and properly insured;

- the supplier will only use staff of a certain calibre to provide the services;

- the supplier will make efforts to prevent any viruses from being introduced into any of the IT systems and will comply with specified security and archiving policies;

- any software used will be millennium and EMU compliant;

- the supplier will comply with all relevant UK and EU laws and the rules and regulations of all governmental agencies and regulatory bodies;

- all deliverables will be accurate and complete.

Term and termination

The duration of the outsourcing deal must be specified. It is also usual to stipulate the date, prior to termination, when both parties review whether they wish to extend the contract or to terminate. The buyer might want to:

- ensure the termination date does not fall during a critical period for the organisation, such as the year end;

- make sure that both parties discuss exit at least six months before the termination date;

- have the right to insist on a transition agreement (*see* Chapter 10);

- have the right to terminate the contract prematurely (if, for instance, the supplier is not performing satisfactorily);

- ensure the contract specifies who should pay the costs arising from termination. This usually varies depending on why the contract is terminated. For example, where the buyer terminates the outsourcing agreement because the supplier is in breach, the supplier should be responsible for most of the costs associated with termination (and vice versa);

- ensure that is has the right to terminate if there is a change in control of its organisation (for instance, if it is the subject of an acquisition or reorganisation and the acquiring company already has in place its own outsourcing arrangements). Similarly the buyer may want to be able to terminate if there is a change of ownership of the supplier and it does not want to be in a contractual relationship with the acquiring company;

- require a right to terminate 'for convenience' – irrespective of whether the supplier is in breach or one of the other termination events has been triggered. A supplier will usually require some form of payment for this right, often calculated on a sliding scale basis, to compensate it for lost earnings potential over the duration of the deal.

No partnership

The term 'partnership' (as described in this book) is used frequently by suppliers. However, buyers will usually want to ensure that a true, legal 'partnership' is not created, as this may lead to fundamental changes to their tax, liability and trading position.

Liabilities

The supplier will usually seek to exclude liability for indirect or consequential losses, but will accept liability for direct losses up to a specified maximum. This means that the supplier would be responsible for the cost of obtaining services which the supplier had failed to provide, but would not be liable for a claim by the buyer that it would have sold £2 m worth of business if its computer systems (operated by the supplier) had not failed. Unfortunately the distinction between direct and consequential losses is not always clear – particularly in the IT field – and it is often advisable to include a non-exhaustive list of the sorts of costs which the parties agree should be recoverable.

Force majeure

While it is generally accepted practice to include a clause excusing failure to perform if this is due to an act beyond the affected party's control, there is often a debate on whether such things as industrial disputes or failures of subcontractors should fall within the definition of 'force majeure'. Clearly from a buyer's perspective this should be resisted.

Confidentiality and data protection

Information is a valuable asset and the supplier must accept an obligation to keep confidential and not disclose to any third party the information about the buyer's clients, suppliers or business of which it becomes aware during the outsourcing. In addition the supplier should accept an obligation to comply with the provisions of the relevant data protection legislation.

Dispute resolution

It is always advisable to include an escalation procedure in the event of a dispute. This forces both parties to consider their position seriously before the matter is referred to an expert, arbitration, conciliation, alternative dispute resolution or the courts for final resolution. Further details are included in Chapter 10.

Exit arrangements

The previous section dealt with the events which trigger a termination and the cost consequences. This section of the contract deals with what happens if a termination event arises. This is a high-risk area for the buyer, but a number of the risks can be reduced by planning ahead in the contract. In particular, provisions should be included to deal with the following.

Exit management plan

It is advisable to require that the supplier create and regularly update an exit management plan which would be activated in the event of a termination or expiry of the contract. The plan is essentially a project plan describing the tasks necessary to 'uncouple' the buyer from the supplier. It should include the assignment of responsibilities for tasks such as transferring licences to the new supplier or to the buyer and implementing the necessary employee consultation procedures. In addition the supplier should keep a register of all of the components of the service, i.e. software, hardware, documentation, skills, facilities and consumables). This register will form the cornerstone of the exit plan and will facilitate the exit arrangements.

Rights to assets

The supplier will have been using its 'know-how' (whether in terms of software, procedures or methodologies) to provide the service – and the buyer will probably need access to this know-how to ensure there is no degradation in service levels after the end of the outsourcing deal. The transition arrangements should therefore provide for the supplier at least to have *access* to these items. There will often be a debate over whether the *ownership* in the intellectual property rights in the know-how should pass to the buyer. This occurs particularly in relation to software developed by the supplier during the course of the outsourcing deal. It is usually recommended that ownership should vest in the buyer, particularly if the software is a crucial component of ongoing service delivery.

For further information on the exit process *see* Chapter 10.

Critical Contract Issues

1   *Description of supplier services.* Is the buyer getting all the services it needs?

2   *Remedies.* Is the supplier adequately penalised for poor performance and can the buyer terminate if service continues to degrade?

3   *Charging mechanism.* Is it clear? Is it consistent with the buyer's deal objectives?

4   *Liabilities.* Are the limits of the buyer's liability at an acceptable level?

5   *Personnel.* People are key to most outsourcing deals – are their concerns addressed?

The negotiation process

There are always many points to discuss in a contract negotiation, but some are more important than others. The buyer must go into the negotiation process knowing which points represent significant elements of outsourcing benefit and risk and what the desired outcome should be. With this information the buyer knows where to focus particular attention.

Two-Stream Negotiation

The negotiation covers the contract and all the schedules. The longest schedule to negotiate is usually the SLA. In some cases buyer and supplier run the SLA negotiation in parallel to the main contract discussions. This can save considerable time but should only be undertaken where the buyer is satisfied that those negotiating on its behalf are qualified to make the relevant decisions on service-related matters and that their work is co-ordinated with that of the main contract negotiating team. (*See* Chapter 8 for more detail.)

Throughout the negotiation process it is essential to maintain a list of buyer risks and benefits. This approach serves several purposes:

- it gives the outsourcing project team a platform to monitor overall progress – this can be very valuable when everyone is embroiled in detailed negotiation;

- it provides a useful way of reporting progress and ultimately the outcome of the negotiation to the decision maker;

- it contributes to the 'risk and benefits' section of the final report to the board;

- it provides the team with a method of gauging its performance at the end of the negotiation; and

- it can be used by internal audit and other groups to monitor project risk and the buyer's overall risk exposure.

Finally, even when the main negotiation is complete, there are usually a number of key issues outstanding. Decision makers from both organisations should meet to agree these final points. The outsourcing project team should brief its decision maker on the remaining issues, the risks posed to the organisation, the supplier's position and the buyer's requirements. Often several issues can be 'bundled' together and offered to the supplier as a complete package, although this 'trading' is not always appropriate. Assuming that these senior figureheads agree the final key points at this meeting, the parties are in a position to have one final review of the draft contract and to sign it.

Key Negotiation Points

1 The objective is to agree a mutually beneficial outcome – not to beat the other side into the ground.

2 Do not start the negotiation process unless you know what you want and what you are willing to concede.

3 Listen carefully to the other side and what they want.

4 Understand the difference, if there is one, between your requirements and theirs.

5 Work through a solution that delivers each side's requirements.

Communications plan

Rumours are more interesting than fact and will be adopted faster than truth.

Crucial to the reduction of risks such as strikes, loss of critical staff, service disruption and a failed outsourcing deal is effective staff communication. Where organisations are unionised and/or where TUPE applies there will be a requirement to consult with employees and union representatives from an early stage.

A communications plan should identify:

- who the main stakeholders are (senior managers and directors, department heads, union representatives, employees, third parties);

- what needs to be communicated to whom;

- when and how often it should be communicated.

Typically, while the contract with the supplier is still being negotiated, the supplier's human resources team will need to meet with buyer staff. These meetings should be attended by both parties' management and must be carefully planned beforehand as sending the wrong message can have a catastrophic effect on the deal.

The communication to staff may comprise:

- reasons for outsourcing;

- which departments and employees it involves;

- which suppliers have been approached;

- a description of the outsourcing process and how far advanced it is (dates are important);

- reasons for not announcing it sooner (this is likely to be the first question);

- what it will mean for staff (positions, terms of employment, pensions);

- when individual staff meetings and counselling sessions will be held;

- the supplier evaluation process;

- what else has been arranged to assist employees understand the effect of the outsourcing on them (e.g. visits to supplier sites, discussions with supplier staff transferred on other client deals);

- methods of submitting questions, highlighting concerns and getting answers (such as a hot line, e-mail box, post box, managers available at certain times).

Regular updates should be scheduled and the schedule never changed. Consistency is very important.

Summary

Contract negotiation is a difficult and time-consuming process. Clarity of the buyer's outsourcing objectives is essential in this phase to keep the outsourcing project team on track. Regardless of how much effort has gone into the outsourcing process up to this point, it will all have been futile if the buyer does not ensure that its requirements are set out clearly in the contract and that it understands the liabilities and other risks which it is exposed to for the duration of the deal. Two of the most important parts of the contract are those that deal with pricing and the SLAs – and these are dealt with in the following chapters.

Ten questions for the team

1   Who is leading the negotiation?

2   What are our most important negotiation points?

3   What is our position on these points and why?

4   What are the key risks in the deal?

5   Does this contract deliver the outsourcing objectives?

6   Does a transition plan exist?

7   When will the transition plan be tested and signed off?

8   What is the fall-back position?

9   What is the procedure for final sign-off?

10   What can we do now that we cannot do once we sign this deal? Is this an acceptable risk?

7

Pricing, bonuses and penalties

Introduction

Two of the most difficult challenges in negotiating an outsourcing deal are agreeing the charges which the buyer will pay for the supplier's services over the life of the deal and agreeing the method which the parties will use to control the performance of those services.

At the outset of the outsourcing deal, the parties agree the price which the supplier will pay to the buyer for the assets to be transferred (such as hardware and contracts) and the service charge which the buyer will pay to the supplier for the outsourced services (as set out in the SLA). Typically the service charge will be calculated using one or more *pricing* or *charging mechanisms*. As the buyer will probably require additional services from the supplier in the future, but cannot define or quantify these at the time of signing the contract, the charging mechanism also needs to be able to provide a method for determining the charges at a future date. A charging mechanism which is agreed at a time when the parties' bargaining power is relatively equal gives the buyer some control over the supplier's charges at a time in the future when it otherwise has little negotiating power.

In the same way that the charging mechanism is used to control future service charges another type of mechanism can be used to influence the supplier's performance with regard to specific services. Typically the parties will negotiate a service *performance mechanism* to penalise or reward supplier performance which respectively exceeds or falls short of an agreed level.

As buyers often cite lack of control over service performance and service charges as two of their key outsourcing concerns it is imperative that mechanisms are built to provide the buyer with the controls that it needs. The first half of this chapter explains the pricing structure of an outsourcing deal and how various charging mechanisms can be employed to control future service charges. The second half describes the mechanisms typically employed by buyers to control service performance in an outsourcing deal and sets out and discusses key issues which often arise with performance mechanisms.

Pricing objectives

All too often the buyer's view is that the pricing objective is for the outsourcing costs to be as low as possible. While this is to an extent true, the reader should consider the following:

- The buyer will need to segregate carefully the transferred functions and processes and the related service charge from any additional services provided by the supplier in the future (which could lead to an apparent rise in the cost of the deal).

- Cost reduction as an objective is likely to clash with the buyer's potential to leverage more value for money from the deal. Some suppliers have been criticised publicly by clients claiming that they were paying considerably more for the outsourced services than they did when the functions or processes were in house. What is not discussed is whether these high outsourcing charges were linked to additional or improved services. Where, for example, a supplier delivers a new system or process previously beyond the capabilities of the buyer, the value to the buyer must be measured in terms other than cost.

- The buyer should also be concerned about the clarity and predictability of charges in addition to the level of the charges.

For the above reasons the pricing objectives of an outsourcing deal should be for the price to:

1 represent value for money;

2 be predictable throughout the life of the deal;

3 be clear and understandable to the buyer.

Charging structures

The various charges payable by both the buyer and the supplier are set out in the following sections of this chapter. The first section describes some of the payments made to the buyer by the supplier in an outsourcing deal; the second deals with the charges levied by the supplier to the buyer (both direct and indirect).

Payments made to the buyer

The subsections below describe the payments which the supplier makes to the buyer and which are usually made at the beginning of an outsourcing deal.

Asset transfer costs

An outsourcing deal often involves the transfer of assets such as facilities, computer hardware and consumables from buyer to supplier. The amount that the supplier pays the buyer for these assets is usually either an estimate of the assets' market value or their book value. Where the buyer has used a conservative depreciation rate the difference between the book value and market value of the assets can be substantial. In this case the buyer has two options. It can either transfer the assets at book value to the supplier, who is likely to charge the difference between book and market value back to the buyer at a later date, or the buyer can transfer the assets at market value and write off the difference in its books. As consideration must be given to accounting standards and the buyer's accounting policy, this decision will be taken by the financial director with advice from internal and/or external audit.

Leasing costs

A growing trend is for assets such as facilities and computer hardware not to be transferred, but instead to be leased to the supplier by the buyer. The advantage to the buyer of this approach is one of control, especially where the contract terminates prematurely and the buyer needs to reclaim its services quickly. The downside for the buyer is that the buyer retains a degree of responsibility for the assets and their maintenance – this can lead to the supplier claiming that the buyer's failure to replace or maintain certain assets resulted in service failures for which the supplier can no longer be held accountable.

Staff charges

Suppliers sometimes seek to charge the buyer for transferring the buyer's staff to the supplier. These transfer charges usually comprise staff relocation costs and administration charges for transferring pensions. However, buyers are quite justified in resisting such charges on the grounds that the staff are a valuable asset and thus the supplier should be responsible for all (or at least a share of) the staff transfer charges.

Incentives

For any number of reasons a supplier might offer a buyer an incentive to sign a specific deal by a specific time. The supplier is perhaps seeking to close the deal before the year end, is anxious to add a prestigious buyer to its client list or sees a particular type of outsourcing deal as important to its future. These cash incentives are usually paid at the beginning of the deal.

Payments made to the supplier

This section is divided into two parts. The first deals with the indirect charges made to the supplier by the buyer. These are the charges for incidental and ancillary items relating to the outsourcing. The second section then deals with the actual charges for the services provided (which are referred to as direct costs).

Some of the indirect charges are as follows:

Records charges

Buyers are often advised to ensure that they have access to registers which list the staff, hardware, software and consumables which the supplier uses to provide the services. This makes the transition task (as described in more detail in Chapter 9) considerably easier for both parties. The supplier, however, may request a charge for the upkeep of the relevant registers.

Termination charges

This group of charges (described in Chapter 9) is usually levied by the supplier for additional work to assist the buyer transfer to another supplier or back in house at the end of the outsourcing deal. Again, the extent of the buyer's liability should be negotiated at the outset of the outsourcing deal.

Novation charges

Where software licences or equipment leases are transferred between the parties at the beginning or end of the outsourcing, costs will be incurred. These have two elements. The first is the legal charge for reviewing the contracts, contacting all of the licensors and lessors and agreeing with them the terms of transfer. The second is the charge, if any, levied by the licensor or lessor to allow the transfer – which can be substantial. At the end of the outsourcing deal the buyer can also incur an increase in licence or lease charges if the supplier enjoyed particularly favourable terms which the licensor or lessor is not willing to extend to the buyer. Buyers should consider these at the outset of the deal and negotiate possible cost-sharing arrangements with their supplier.

Intellectual property

If the supplier amends or creates software on behalf of the buyer during the life of the outsourcing deal, the ownership of the resulting intellectual property rights needs to be clarified in the outsourcing contract. If the supplier owns the intellectual property it may charge the buyer to transfer those rights to it or a third party at the end of the deal.

Bidding charges

Where the cost to the supplier to bid for the outsourcing deal is very high the supplier may seek to recover these costs. Bidding costs can at times be in excess of £1 m.

Tax charges

In the UK some sectors whose services to their clients are VAT exempt cannot recover the VAT which they themselves pay for services. This is particularly the case with financial services. Where buyers are required to pay VAT on the supplier's charges they will need to make provision for these additional charges. A potential way of avoiding this liability which is sometimes employed is to set up a joint venture with the supplier and transfer resources and assets from both parties into the joint venture organisation rather than to the supplier. Since the joint venture organisation is still part of the buyer organisation there is an argument that the service charges do not incur VAT. However, the joint venture organisation can be costly and cumbersome to set up and manage. It should be stressed that this is a complex issue which is affected by a number of variables. An analysis of these issues is beyond the scope of this book and accordingly expert VAT advice should be sought.

Relocation charges

Where the supplier chooses to move its operation to another location it may seek to charge the buyer for some of the relocation costs. Even when a buyer is not directly charged there may be indirect costs such as extra telecommunications charges resulting from a more remote supplier site. Whether a relocation by the supplier should cost the buyer more is an issue for the parties themselves and is a scenario which should be dealt with in the contract.

Service charges

In addition to these indirect charges there are a number of charges directly related to the services which the supplier provides to the buyer. For several reasons (described later), these service charges are best considered in terms of the three following areas of activity typically found in an outsourcing deal:

- *operating services* – running or operating the functions or processes transferred to the supplier by the buyer;
- *enhancement services* – services requested when the buyer wishes to make a change to the operating services;
- *new services* – services called on by the buyer when it wants to commission a project to deliver a new service to its users.

The characteristics of each of these groups of services are set out in Table 7.1. It is important to understand these different characteristics as they affect they type of pricing mechanism used to control them.

Table 7.1
Types of direct service charge

	Operating services	Enhancement services	New services
Description	Operation of and minor changes to outsourced functions and processes	Changes to existing operating services	New projects to deliver new services
Examples	Operating an IT system	Year 2000 Enhancements of current IT systems	Commission of a work-flow imaging system
	Operating financial services claims processing	Large process enhancement project	New back-office processes
Skills type required	Known Transferred to supplier	Known	Unknown
Skills quantity required	Known (may vary) Transferred to supplier	Unknown	Unknown
Software required (type and quantity)	Known	Partially known	Unknown
Technology required (type and quantity)	Known Transferred to supplier	Known (probably)	Unknown
Predictability of future charge at outset of deal	Considerable	Partial	Very little

The risk for a buyer of not securing a future charge which is predictable and which represents value for money increases as one moves from left to right on the table. The risk for the supplier also increases since it might give guarantees of its capability where the future cost of complying with such a requirement cannot be calculated. If, for example, a supplier guaranteed its client that it would provide world-class finance skills for the life of the deal, the risk that the supplier cannot honour this guarantee increases over the life of the outsourcing deal as its ability to predict what in the future will constitute 'world-class finance skills' reduces over time.

Fundamentally the objectives of the buyer and supplier are in conflict in relation to the charging mechanism. The buyer will want to fix as many of the charges up front, whether for operating, enhancement or new services. By contrast, the supplier will want to retain as much flexibility as possible, particularly in relation to enhancement and new services, as it will want to avoid making commitments about future performance at a time when it cannot fully assess the cost implications. At the very minimum a supplier is likely to require that the rates specified for at least some elements of the service are linked to an appropriate index (such as RPI).

The charging mechanism

The objective of a charging mechanism is to make sure that the price paid represents value for money, is understandable (in terms of what it covers and what is excluded) and is as predictable as possible. The charging mechanism should also take into account the value which the supplier brings to the deal, whether through cost reduction, service improvement or both.

As explained above, the charging mechanisms used for different groups of services and even different services in the same group will depend on the specific service or service group objectives set by the buyer and the information available at the time the charging mechanism is agreed. The information required is outlined in Figure 7.1, along with an indication of its availability at the time the charging mechanism is constructed.

Figure 7.1
Information required to set up the outsourcing charging mechanism

Information	Operate	Enhance	New
Services that the buyer requires	✓	✓	✗
Components of those services and their costs and their relationship to service volume and changes in service volume	✓	?	✗
Amount of service (including geographic spread) required	✓	?	✗
Service performance required	✓	✗	✗
Supplier's profit margin and where it will be added	✓	✓	✗
Value which the supplier is adding (which may be part of the above – *see* next section)	✓	✓	?
Key ✓ = information known at time of contract signing; ✗ = information unknown at time of contract signing; ? = information possibly known at time of contract signing.			

No two outsourcing deals are the same, so giving specific recommendations is hazardous, but it is useful to understand the most commonly encountered charging mechanisms. The following subsections therefore give an indication of these key mechanisms. Since the type of charging mechanism is likely to vary depending on the type of service to which it applies, each of the three groups of services is then considered in terms of the most likely applicable charging mechanism.

Input pricing

This mechanism is often referred to as *cost plus* pricing. In essence the charge is based on the supplier's costs in providing the services, plus the supplier's profit margin.

The cost plus mechanism ensures maximum visibility of service cost and supplier profit for the buyer. However, it also involves a considerable risk for the buyer as it has little control over the costs which the supplier incurs and there is no incentive for the supplier to reduce costs or to restrict the volume of services ordered by the buyer's user groups. In addition the buyer will need to police the supplier's input costs throughout the life of the deal to ensure that all costs are validly incurred and are properly chargeable to the buyer – and this can be a very costly exercise.

Controls can, however, be applied to input pricing mechanisms to give greater protection for buyers. It is always advisable to limit the categories of costs which can be incurred and to impose obligations on the supplier to provide the services in the most cost-effective manner possible. The elements of the charges must be backed up by appropriate documentation (such as third-party invoices) and the buyer should be able to audit all relevant books and data. In addition, it is also possible to agree target costs for the services, so that if the supplier's actual costs exceed (or are less than) this target an appropriate division of the resulting variance can be agreed. Thus the supplier would be expected to pick up increasingly larger amounts of any cost overruns, but would also be awarded the greater share of any cost reductions. This provides a valuable incentive for the supplier to reduce the buyer's costs and to ensure cost-effective service utilisation.

Output pricing

This can be divided further into the following categories (although the list is by no means exhaustive).

Transaction processing

The buyer and supplier can agree on a mechanism for calculating the service charge (including the supplier profit margin) per unit of the service delivered. This unit is often referred to as a transaction and the calculation method the *transaction charging* mechanism. As the charge is based on the end result of the service rather than the cost components which make it up, this method is an example of *output pricing*. While the charge for a transaction may be calculated at the outset of the outsourcing deal by determining the overall cost to provide the service, adding the supplier's profit and dividing the total by the number of transactions (which mirrors the cost plus mechanism previously discussed), as the transaction price is then fixed (and not variable with changes to the supplier's input prices), it is a far less risky approach from the buyer's perspective. The cost per transaction can then be compared over time with an industry standard cost to benchmark the supplier's performance. However, where external benchmarking information is not available it is more difficult for the buyer to ensure that the supplier is providing value for money.

An example of a transaction charging mechanism might be a payroll processing service where the buyer pays a flat fee of £1.60 per payslip per month for 10 000 payslips. This figure also includes end-of-year payroll processing (P35 returns etc.) and a number of payroll changes (adding new employees etc.) per annum. Charges are also specified for additional changes or increases to the overall volume of payslips.

Transaction charging mechanisms provide the supplier with the incentive to focus on reducing the cost of service components and also on optimising the mix of the components. Buyers relinquish control over the component costs and the supplier's profit in return for a cost-effective transaction charge. An additional advantage of transaction-based charging is that, where the buyer can ascertain volume usage by different departments within its own organisation, it can easily calculate an internal service charge for each department, thereby increasing user accountability for service consumption. However, as with cost plus charging mechanisms, the supplier is not given an incentive to reduce the volume of transactions (unless specific provision is made for this).

Transaction charges have the advantage of making it easier to assess the effects of volume changes on the overall price for a service. However, it is also common to see the introduction of usage bands or volume limits. These are often favoured by buyers who wish to ensure that they are not exposed to extra charges when their service requirements increase at certain times (such as the year end) and by suppliers who do not want to reduce their exposure to revenue fluctuations in periods of low service usage.

Productivity pricing

This approach involves specifying productivity level requirements. Using an IT example, software development productivity is often measured using a function point, which essentially establishes a price for a number of lines of bug-free programming code. Function points can be difficult to use but when employed correctly they allow a buyer in an outsourcing deal to 'buy' a certain quantity of function points from a supplier, thereby removing the buyer's need to be concerned about any of the supplier's costs (such as the number of programmers used). The obvious difficulty of using function points is that the supplier is not given an incentive to keep the computer programs short since its income is a function of the number of function points (or lines of computer program) that it produces. This issue is partially dealt with by negotiating with the supplier at the time of requesting the service the number of function points required. Where the supplier requires more than the agreed number the buyer is not charged, or charged at a lower rate. The advantage for organisations using function points is that, to a degree, the charge for function points can be benchmarked against other organisations.

Most likely charging mechanism

Having looked briefly at the key charging mechanisms, we now consider how the use of these different mechanisms is likely to change depending on which of the three types of service is being priced.

Operating services

At least initially operating services involve operating the function or process which the buyer transfers to the supplier. Such services are often charged on a transaction pricing basis. However, a considerable amount of information will be required during contract negotiation to be able to construct a meaningful and effective mechanism. Where some or all of the information set out in Figure 7.1 is not available the buyer is more restricted in its choice of mechanism.

One variant of transaction pricing is for the parties to agree on a charging mechanism which rewards the supplier by a percentage of the cost savings that it makes for the buyer. For this to be effective both parties need to have access to detailed information about the current cost to the buyer of operating the service. It is also an approach which needs to be carefully thought through to make sure the cost reductions do not lead to an unacceptable decline in service levels.

Enhancement services

Enhancement services span a wide range of supplier services, including the provision of an existing operating service in a new location and implementing a large IT conversion project to make systems millennium compliant. It is assumed, however, that these 'changes' relate to the services which the supplier is currently operating and therefore the skills and expertise required are broadly predictable, even though the quantity is not.

Because of the difficulty of predicting the volumes required, enhancement services are often priced on a cost plus or productivity basis. A variant of these mechanisms would be to adopt a 'call-off' approach. This involves the buyer specifying the resources and assets that can be called off and if possible giving some indication of volume requirements. The buyer and supplier will probably negotiate an input cost level at this point, setting out charges for specific volumes of specific skills as and when they are required in the future. In the case of people skills, particularly in countries where there is steep wage inflation, the supplier will tie the charging mechanism into a skills price index. In a pure cost plus arrangement, the supplier may not have the incentive to source skills in cheaper countries or to restrict its usage of skills on a particular project.

New services

Where a buyer requires a new service from a supplier during the outsourcing deal it is unlikely to know at the outset of the deal what that service will be or the type or quantity of skills and assets required. This means that transaction pricing is likely to be difficult or impossible to apply. In some cases broad productivity and resource charges can be agreed and commitments can be sought from suppliers to provide assets, such as technology, at a price which is related to an industry 'best price' for that asset.

The charging mechanism is often decided at the time the service is requested. The buyer can at best set out at the time of contract negotiation a mechanism for arriving at a charging mechanism in the future. This might involve agreeing to look to nominated third parties for assistance or seeking competitive bids for that particular project, the objective of the latter option being to give the supplier a benchmark against which it must match its charge.

Bonus and penalty regimes

Many outsourcing deals contain a bonus and penalty regime which is intended to reward the supplier for above contracted levels of performance and penalise the supplier for below anticipated levels of performance. Suppliers often do not favour penalty regimes as they believe that they sour the buyer–supplier partnership and can be costly. As buyers legitimately expect their suppliers to perform at or above the contracted service levels, some feel that bonus regimes are superfluous as the supplier's reward is already contained in the service charge. However, there are benefits to both sides in such schemes and they are found in most deals. Both bonuses and penalties are generally expected to be financial in nature and it is assumed in this section that the regimes relate to services the performance of which is not already linked to the supplier's income through a profit-sharing mechanism.

Decision makers must understand the effect that these regimes have on outsourcing deals. If one or both regimes are used, the outsourcing team needs to put an effective structure in place. Both decision makers and the outsourcing team need to consider carefully the issues surrounding the bonus and penalty regimes and ensure that they are not working against the objectives of the outsourcing deal.

This section explains the objectives of bonus and penalty regimes, describes a process for constructing the regimes and finally discusses problems which are commonly encountered when building and operating bonus and penalty regimes.

Objectives

If the sole objective of a bonus and penalty regime is to reward good supplier performance or punish failure to achieve certain goals, then the buyer can expect limited success. Where the objective is to provide the supplier with the incentive to focus its attention on specific buyer services and to influence the supplier's behaviour with regard to those services, then both parties are likely to come considerably closer to achieving the objectives of the outsourcing deal.

A buyer must first decide whether the effort of implementing bonus and penalty regimes in their outsourcing deal is justifiable. To do this they must consider:

- whether there are services within the portfolio which, from the perspective of the buyer's business users, would benefit from superlative supplier performance;
- whether there are services within the portfolio which, again from the perspective of the buyer's business users, would suffer from substandard supplier performance;
- in the case of a bonus regime, whether they are willing to finance such a scheme;
- how many services should be included within the bonus and/or penalty regime;
- what the cost of measurement is, i.e. whether any special measurement tools are required and what the anticipated staff cost is of maintaining the regime;

- what the expected benefits of attaching penalties and/or bonuses to the specific services might be, both in terms of the services themselves and other services which do not fall under the regime. It is sometimes the case that a bonus or penalty regime can detract attention from other services and have a negative impact on their performance.

Where the decision maker, having considered the above points, can see concrete reasons for using a bonus and penalty regime it will need to agree with the supplier the structure of the regime to be implemented.

Structure

The structure of a bonus and penalty regime in an outsourcing deal must be considered at two levels. The first, the macro level, defines the structure of the regime across the outsourcing deal, including issues such as setting a cap on the penalty and/or bonus payments incurred by both sides. The second, the micro level, deals with structural considerations at the level of the specific services which will be covered by the regime.

Macro-level structure

Where the buyer and supplier agree that bonus and penalty regimes should be included in their outsourcing deal, they will need to consider the following:

Capping – It is recommended that a limit be imposed on the amount of the bonus or penalty which can be incurred in a specified period. Generally the limit for both bonuses and penalties can be set as a percentage of the supplier's annual service charge. Penalties are generally limited to the amount of profit that the supplier is making on the outsourcing deal – usually in the region of 10 to 25 per cent. There are cases where the penalty limit extends beyond the profit level to as much as 40 per cent of the annual service charge, but generally buyers see the sense in ensuring that their supplier is not driven into a loss-making situation as a result of the penalty regime. The bonus limit is usually below that of the penalty – often the starting point for negotiation is approximately 5 per cent of the supplier's annual service charge. However, as with the penalty limit, the precise amount is case specific.

Charging period – Both parties will need to agree the measurement and payment period for bonuses and penalties, the options being monthly, quarterly, half yearly or yearly. Frequently the parties will choose to measure performance and calculate penalty and bonus payments on a monthly or quarterly basis since frequent attention to service performance is likely to result in more rapid implementation of any necessary service changes. Payment of bonuses and penalties typically occur either quarterly or annually. It is usually advisable to ensure that payments are made as soon as possible after the bonus or penalty was incurred so that the effect of the supplier's performance is more visible to both parties.

Cross period accounting – Bonus and penalty caps are often initially set as an annual sum. In the case where measurement and payment occur more than once in the year the buyer will need to decide whether penalties and/or bonuses are capped in the measurement period and, if the supplier exceeds that limit, whether the excess bonus or penalty should be carried into the next period. In the case of penalties the concern often expressed by buyers is that where a supplier incurs all of its annual penalty limit in the first quarter of the year, the regime will have little influence on the supplier for the remainder of the year. The same applies to bonus regimes. It is often best to apportion a penalty or bonus limit to a period, e.g. monthly or quarterly, and to start each period anew. This approach, coupled with the recommendation made in the section on penalty and bonus regime issues below, should ensure that both parties' attention to service delivery and performance is more balanced throughout the year.

Measurement system – A difficulty with bonus and penalty regimes is that service performance, whether measured as the achievement of a cost reduction or improvement in service delivery, must be expressed in a way which can be equated to an amount of the bonus or penalty allocated. Often the parties implement a points mechanism which is not dissimilar to an airline air miles incentive scheme where the reward for various types of activity, whether travelling a certain distance, staying in a specific hotel or hiring a car from a designated car hire firm, are all converted to a common points scheme. The allocation of points to services is described below in the section on the micro-level structure. To avoid an administrative nightmare each point should have equal monetary value and that value should be set out in the outsourcing contract. Where the parties need to adjust the bonus or penalty limits in the outsourcing deal they can do this simply by changing the monetary value of a point.

Critical services – As already stated in the section on objectives above, the buyer must decide which services which it will include in the bonus and/or penalty regime. In an attempt to keep the administrative overhead to a minimum it is recommended that the set of services is limited to those where there is a clear benefit to the buyer's service users in applying a bonus or penalty regime. As the emphasis which service users will attach to specific services is likely to change during the life of the outsourcing deal, it is advisable that the buyer stipulates in the outsourcing contract that the set of services to be measured can be changed at certain intervals. For example, where a new service is commissioned during the outsourcing deal which is very important to the buyer's organisation the buyer may wish to add this service to the regime in place of an older one.

Monitoring and reporting – A danger with bonus and penalty regimes is that great effort is expended in structuring the regime, only for the operation of it to be neglected during the life of the outsourcing deal. Both parties should set out in the outsourcing contract the responsibilities for the periodic measurement and reporting of the service performance and the bonus and penalty points incurred. It is recommended that, at a senior management level, both parties meet at least once a year to review the effectiveness of the bonus and penalty regime and to agree any amendments to the regime.

Micro-level structure

There are a number of key decisions specific to each service in the bonus and/or penalty regime which the buyer must take:

Services – Which precise outputs or components of each service will be measured in the regime? Where do those outputs occur and when? For example, an insurance organisation which provides motor insurance to clients might find that a considerable amount of its annual revenue is taken by telephone on the first Monday of each month (assuming many buyers purchase cars just after receiving their end-of-month pay cheque). If the insurance organisation outsources its policy booking system to a third party it will want to ensure that the relevant system is available during those critical Monday mornings. The regime will therefore stipulate that System X is available to the policy booking staff for specified hours on the first Monday of each month. Clearly the system is important on other days too, but only the critical availability described above may be included in the bonus and/or penalty regime.

Measurement – Having defined the service outputs for inclusion in the regime, the buyer will decide what measures to use and how. It is important that the measures clearly demonstrate whether the desired service performance is achieved or not. To illustrate this point consider a telephone booking service which airlines provide for customers who wish to book and pay for air tickets. If the call centre is measured by the time it takes to answer the phone, then the call centre will achieve its objective and may even be rewarded with a performance bonus if it routes a caller with a difficult request from one operative to another – as long as the operatives all pick up the telephone within a specified number of rings. However, the true performance measure is probably the time required to take a caller's booking – and the call centre may be failing dismally to meet this measure.

Buyers must define what 'normal' achievement is in order to have a baseline against which they can determine superlative and substandard performance. To do this they will need to have historical measurement data. Where these do not exist the supplier will probably recommend a measurement moratorium during which both parties will monitor the services and form a view as to what is a realistic performance level.

Once measures have been determined and agreed by both parties, a conversion mechanism will be built to transform the measurement results into points, which will in turn ultimately be expressed as a monetary value. For example a penalty point may be incurred for every minute that System X (described in the example of the insurance organisation) is unavailable during the critical time. A bonus point may be received for every customer whose insurance policy is set up within three minutes on the telephone. The parties will also need to decide whether points will accumulate for a prolonged failure or improvement, or whether the bonus or penalty points are incurred as a one-off on the occurrence of an event, irrespective of the duration of the event. The decision is clearly based on the type of service which is being measured, how poor or good performance affects the buyer's business and the way in which the buyer wishes the supplier to behave once an event has occurred. For example, where an airline telephone booking does not occur within four minutes of the call being answered the buyer may choose to penalise the supplier with a one-off penalty of, say, 5 points. By contrast, in the case of the insurance company where every minute the booking system is down has more and more impact on the buyer's revenue stream, the buyer may choose to impose a penalty which accumulates with time and even becomes exponentially more severe after a certain amount of time.

Penalty and bonus regime issues

It should be apparent by now that there are a number of dynamics in operation in bonus and penalty regimes and that trade-offs often need to be made to achieve an effective regime. The following are some of the issues and trade-offs of which buyers and suppliers should be aware.

Cost versus points

There are some cases where the cost of incurring a penalty is less onerous to the supplier than the cost of performing the relevant service. A good example of this is business continuity planning and testing. Many outsourcing contracts stipulate that one of the services which the supplier should provide is to test regularly (half yearly or yearly) that its services can be transferred to another site and function in the event of a disaster.

Since this is a critical service and it is imperative that planning and testing occur frequently, some buyers place the service within the penalty regime. Where the supplier fails to carry out the necessary tests it would incur a number of penalty points. The difficulty with this is that more often than not the cost of doing the test exceeds the value of the penalty points for not conducting the test. If the buyer were to increase the number of points for such a failure it would eat into the overall cap on penalties in the contract, thus leaving the buyer without a remedy for other critical service failures covered by the penalty scheme. For this reason, it is recommended that such services are not included in the bonus and/or penalty regime. As an alternative, failure to provide a critical service could be categorised as a breach of contract, thus giving the buyer the opportunity to sue for damages at large.

Bonus and penalty – mutually exclusive

Some buyers stipulate that where a supplier incurs a penalty in a certain period it also foregoes all rights to any bonus points which it earned in the same period. Where several distinct services are provided by different supplier teams and the bonus points relate in some way to their personal bonus schemes, removing all teams' bonuses due to the failure of one team might seem inequitable to the others and might only serve to demotivate staff who were previously performing well.

Staff rewards

The bonus payments made to suppliers are often quite small compared with the overall size of the outsourcing deal. Some suppliers choose to channel any bonuses earned on a particular outsourcing deal directly to the staff who operate that deal. This not only serves to motivate staff involved with the deal, but also makes that deal a particularly attractive one to work on for employees within the supplier's organisation.

Buyer attitude

There is a danger that some buyers will treat penalty regimes as a potential revenue stream. Regarding it as such essentially incites the buyer to encourage the supplier to fail. One method of dealing with this is to link the performance of the contract management team (discussed in Chapter 9) to the supplier's performance.

Non-financial remedies

Financial penalties and bonuses at best only recompense the buyer for service failure – they will not necessarily solve service failure or poor performance issues. The reason for this is that there is little guarantee that once a supplier incurs a penalty the failure will not recur. While the penalty regime provides the supplier with an incentive not to fail and to ensure in the future that failures do not recur, the penalty cap is often so low that it is easier for a supplier to allow certain problems to recur than to resolve them. One solution is for the contract to provide that where a certain number of penalty points is exceeded in a period, or levels are unsatisfactory over several consecutive periods, senior managers from the supplier should meet with the buyer and report on:

- the cause of the repetitive failures or poor performance;
- the action to be taken to ensure these failures are resolved for the future;
- how and when the effects of these remedies will be reported to the buyer.

These non-financial remedies can be very effective and can deliver an end result of improved service which surpasses what can be achieved by the financial penalty scheme alone.

Supplier behaviour

Bonus and/or penalty regimes affect supplier behaviour. If a call centre operative is rewarded by the speed at which he or she can process customer calls, then it should come as no surprise to the buyer if the employee is irritating customers by rushing them through a call and sometimes not completing call processes properly. The solution to this problem is often to issue rules to employees which run counter to the very behaviour that the bonus regime promotes. Setting rules can confuse staff and result in substandard services. It is recommended that buyers and suppliers spend some time when implementing the bonus and/or penalty regime in considering what types of behaviour are likely to result from the schemes – and if such behaviour is desirable.

Summary

Pricing the outsourcing deal continues to be a significant challenge. It is not only critical for the organisation to get a 'good' price but also to get the pricing mechanism which best suits the objectives of their outsourcing deal. It is unlikely that one pricing mechanism will satisfy all the requirements of an outsourcing deal since a typical deal will comprise many different types of work. Additionally, the buyer will, at the outset of the outsourcing deal, lack some of the information necessary to create the pricing mechanisms it would ultimately desire. In the case of pricing mechanisms for new developments which may not occur for several years, it may only be possible to agree a scheme for deciding a mechanism at a later date.

Closely linked to the pricing mechanism is the bonus and penalty regime. These regimes are difficult to get right and both parties need to consider a number of issues before implementing them. Ultimately a poorly thought out bonus and/or penalty regime can motivate the supplier to perform in a way which contradicts the buyer's service objectives.

Ten recommendations when building bonus and penalty regimes

1   Decide whether bonus and/or penalty regimes are needed.

2   Pick the key services to which they should apply (bonus and penalty regimes need not apply to the same services).

3   Pick the outputs of those services that are critical to the business and are measurable.

4   Determine the 'normal', 'above normal' and 'below normal' levels of required service.

5   Choose the regime structure.

6   Choose the monitoring system.

7   Assess the effect of the regime on staff performance.

8   Determine the cap on bonus and incentive payments.

9   Apply and monitor the regime – do not let it fall into disuse.

10   Regularly review and update the regime to reflect changes in outsourcing objectives.

8

Create strong service level agreements

Introduction

The service level agreement (SLA) is the backbone of an outsourcing deal. The SLA describes all of the services which the buyer is purchasing from the supplier, the measures used to monitor the service delivery and the target performance levels. Penalty and bonus schemes many also be defined to penalise and reward deviations from the performance targets respectively. During the life of the contract the SLA, which evolves to cater for changes to the service portfolio, is a mechanism which the buyer can use to retain a degree of control over the service. And finally, at the end of the contract life, the SLA should be a reference for understanding what the supplier is likely to return to the buyer – should the buyer choose not to renew the contract.

Buyers are often concerned by their loss of control over services once an outsourcing deal is signed. There will undoubtedly be a degree of loss of control, but adequate control must be retained and this is achieved by using strong SLAs and a dedicated service management team. Strong SLAs define clearly *what* a service delivers, *when* it is delivered and *where* it is delivered to. It should not be allowed to deviate into a description of *how* the service is delivered. Additionally, strong SLAs are controlled by using a few effective measures which ideally are meaningful to the service users and relate in some way to the service price.

Often, however, buyers enter outsourcing agreements with less than adequate or a total absence of SLAs – opening their organisations to unnecessarily high levels of risk as a result of weak service control. When the deal is being prepared it is often difficult for both sides to maintain the focus necessary to prepare a strong SLA. Drafting an SLA is a time-consuming exercise. The time and resource required often deters buyers from preparing SLAs or forces them to restrict the effort, resulting in less than adequate agreements. It is common for suppliers to take on the SLA drafting role – estimated in the KPMG survey[1] to occur in about 50 per cent of all deals. But suppliers are also less than enthusiastic about having strong SLAs included in the contract as they may prove too onerous. The result is a weak SLA which in turn can mean a very weak deal – a deal in which the buyer relinquishes ownership of critical services without ensuring that a control mechanism is in place.

This chapter highlights the threats to buyers and suppliers of not having strong SLAs in place at the start of a deal. It presents a number of sections, describing one or more of the key problem areas and making recommendations to resolve or avoid these problems. Finally, some commonly encountered concerns regarding SLAs are discussed and best-practice tips are given.

---

1.   *The Maturing of Outsourcing* (London: KPMG, 1997).

Failure to produce SLAs

If SLAs are not produced there is no agreement about the services that the supplier will provide, the metrics which will be used to measure their performance or the performance objectives for the various services. The resulting risks are as follows:

- The supplier has a poor understanding of the buyer's requirement, leading to potentially poor service performance and even service disruption.

- The buyer and supplier may have differing views as to what is within the scope of the deal. The risk for the buyer is a series of additional costs in order to bring vital services into scope. The risk for the supplier is a very disgruntled client from the outset of the contract and poor publicity.

- The buyer, if operating in a regulated industry, many have difficulty in proving that it has adequate control over its outsourced services (*see* the section on control in Chapter 4 for more details).

- Finally, it will prove difficult at the end of the contract to understand what services 'belong' to the buyer, should it wish to retrieve them. Ultimately the risk is that it will be locked into its current supplier when such an arrangement is no longer beneficial.

Timing

The key question is whether the SLA will be completed before the deal is signed. There are two primary reasons for recommending that the SLA is completed before the contract is signed. The first is that the buyer is in a considerably stronger position to ensure that *all* of its service requirements are reflected in the SLA. Waiting until after contract signature is almost guaranteed to lead to disputes regarding the scope of the agreement. The second is that there is a risk that the SLA will never be completed once the contract is signed as buyer and supplier staff refocus attention on ensuring a smooth service transition and continued ongoing service delivery.

Drafting the SLA

It is usually recommended that the drafting of the SLA is led by the buyer with assistance from the supplier. Often, however, the supplier offers to take on this time- and resource-intensive activity. In this situation the buyer risks:

- getting a less onerous SLA in terms of supplier obligations;

- having to pay the supplier for the exercise;

- not focusing the SLA on buyer requirements and service priorities;

- losing the opportunity for the buyer's contract management team to be heavily involved in defining the services which it will at a later stage then manage.

However, the risk of not securing an adequate SLA is not entirely removed even if the buyer is in control of the SLA drafting process. Two further steps are required. The first is for the buyer to ensure that the supplier is involved. This will ensure supplier familiarity with the services before contract signing. The second is that service users must be involved in the preparation of the SLA. They will receive the service so they should have a say in what they will get. Buyers sometimes contend that user involvement would add a considerable time burden to SLA drafting. This may be true, but involvement should reduce subsequent disputes with service users.

Describe services not procedures

Too often SLAs describe *how* the service is performed or provided rather than *what* the service delivers. Defining only the *how* (i.e. the procedure to achieve the *what*, rather than the *what* itself) presents a number of risks for the outsourcing deal:

- The SLA can be unnecessarily restrictive for the supplier. On the one hand the buyer wants the supplier to use its existing skills, knowledge and experience to provide a particular service; on the other hand it wants to prescribe to the supplier how the supplier should do its job.

- The buyer still has not defined what service outputs it is to receive from the supplier, which in turn can foster a mismatch in supplier/buyer expectations.

- The buyer's knowledge and expertise in providing a particular service will diminish with time as the supplier takes over the supply role and the buyer's staff transfer to the supplier. *How*-based SLAs will become meaningless at the same time.

- The size of the SLA becomes huge, as does the resource and time investment required to produce what is essentially a procedures manual.

Describing *what* the service delivers is considerably more difficult for those preparing the SLA than describing *how* the service is performed. The latter is merely a description of the activities comprising a department's daily routine. Soliciting the assistance of service users can be very useful here as they generally find it easier to describe *what* they get rather than *how* they get it. The service definition should, in addition, describe *when* and *where* the service is delivered. A good example of this is part of a payroll service. *What:*

a pay cheque. *Where:* to my home address. *When:* on the last Thursday of the month. *How:* don't care![2]

A frequent counter-argument to this approach is that relinquishing the definition of *how* the service is provided means that the buyer loses control over the supplier. This is true to an extent but outsourcing does involve a shift in operational control to the supplier. The recommendation is to focus on *what* is delivered in the SLA. If a buyer wishes to control how its supplier performs a service, the overhead to the buyer in setting up such control is likely to challenge the value of using a third-party supplier – as some organisations have found to their cost.

Clarify service boundaries

The risk with not knowing where one party's responsibility ends and the other's starts typically leads to disputes between buyer and supplier, or between several suppliers and the buyer in multi-supplier arrangements. In either case the buyer loses out. If service outputs are defined very clearly in terms of *what*, *when* and *where* the service is to be delivered, the chance of disputes about the scope of the outsourcing deal is substantially reduced.

Define all of the services

Based on the premise that the buyer is only entitled to receive the services set out in the SLA, this aspect is obviously very important, but it is difficult to ensure the SLA is comprehensive. The risk is that the buyer does not get what it expects and will be forced to pay extra to have the missing services introduced through the change management process. Only checking and double checking the SLA with a good cross-section of the service user community can reduce this risk.

In addition to describing the services which the supplier will provide to the buyer, the SLA should also define the 'background' or 'indirect' services which the supplier will supply as part of managing the overall service provision. These services are of most concern to the buyer's contract management staff (rather than the users). Examples of indirect services include service invoicing, service monitoring and service reporting. These are described in more detail in Chapter 9.

---

2. This approach is described in far more detail in the KPMG's SLA Guide publication number 5830 (London: KPMG, 1997), available on request.

Define service performance measures

Best practice recommends that performance measures should be readily understandable to service users and help gauge achievement of the service objectives. Additionally, the cost of measuring should not exceed the benefit. The risk, for both parties, of not using any performance measures can be a mismatch of buyer/supplier expectations.

Applying measures to almost every service can be costly to set up and maintain, and the cost of so many measures may far outstrip the benefit they provide. Focusing on a few important and meaningful measures is often more advantageous than using a multiplicity which can become meaningless after a short while. Again, users must be involved in identifying the service outputs and measures which are key to the operation of their business.

It is often the case that prior to entering into the outsourcing deal buyers did not have in place a measurement mechanism for the services which they now wish the supplier to measure. This poses two problems for the buyer. The first is that the supplier will probably require payment to set up the mechanism. The second is that the buyer does not have any historic data upon which to base supplier performance expectations. Normally the supplier will request a three- to six-month measurement moratorium during which it will set up the measurement mechanism and will gather data. At the end of the agreed period the parties will use the data to agree future performance targets. Service performance penalties and bonuses will not usually apply until the end of the moratorium.

In-depth analysis of the types of measures available is beyond the scope of this publication.

Frequently encountered SLA issues

Penalty and bonus regimes in SLAs

This is an extremely complex area which has been addressed in detail in the previous chapter. However, as the penalty and bonus regime is so pivotal to an SLA, some of the key issues are highlighted again in the following paragraphs.

Service 'penalties' or credits are often applied to specific services to penalise the supplier for below-expected levels of performance. Bonuses reward the supplier for above-'normal' levels of performance. A reward/penalty mechanism is useful to focus a supplier on those services which are critical to the buyer's business. For example, a supermarket chain which uses third-party information technology services may wish to structure penalties around the unavailability of store systems during peak shopping times.

As penalties and bonuses can shape the behaviour of the supplier and have significant impact on an outsourcing deal, careful consideration must be given to the design of the regime. Chapter 7 contains a detailed discussion on penalty and bonus regimes. For the purposes of SLAs it is worth re-capping under four headings:

Services

This covers the specific services to which penalties and/or bonuses will apply. These should be services for which tangible business loss or benefit can be demonstrated as a result of sub- or super-normal service performance. When considered in this way the number of critical services can often be restricted. Consideration must, however, also be given to those services outside of the regime which may 'suffer' as a result of the bias in the supplier's focus.

Metrics

This covers the types of service performance measure. Metrics must align specifically with the objectives of the service. By way of example, consider the following scenario. An insurance company set up an SLA for its call centre. The call centre was responsible for handling clients' claims and comprised first- and second-level claims processing groups. Level one took the call and tried to resolve the claim. Complex claims which would take longer to resolve were forwarded for level two attention. Level one staff were given substantial bonuses depending on the number of calls they processed. The resultant behaviour: all claims were sent to level two as level one staff tried to move clients on as quickly as possible in order to take a new call. Level two became heavily overloaded. The solution was to change the bonus structure to include metrics like 'the number of claims resolved' (whether by levels one or two).

Performance

This covers the definition of 'good' and 'poor' performance. Penalty/bonus regimes must focus on poor and good performance, not 'normal' performance for which the buyer already pays the service charge. Poor and good must be defined in the context of business loss and business benefit. If the aforementioned insurance company processes more claims per day and thus has a higher than normal outgoings because of super-normal call-centre staff performance, they should be given bonuses. Finally, performance targets should only be set with access to at least three to six months of historical measurement data. Statistical models can be used to predict probable penalty and bonus payments.

Charges

This covers the frequency and method of charging. Questions here arise around the issue of accumulating penalties. What if a supplier incurs all of the service credits up to the agreed annual cap in the first month of service provision: is there an incentive to perform well for the rest of the year? If more than the capped amount is incurred in a period, should the difference be carried forward? The issue here is that poor performance can continue long after a financial cap has been exhausted. This 'gap' is best filled with non-financial stipulations, for instance requiring a senior member of the supplier organisation to visit the buyer as soon as possible to explain:

- reasons for the poor performance;

- measures being taken to ensure immediate performance improvement;

- measures to prevent a future recurrence of the failures.

One supplier suggested that bonus payments should be made directly to staff. While this approach has merit in so far as it makes service performance more visible to the relevant staff, careful consideration must be given to the possible HR issues, including demotivating staff outside of the bonus scheme and possible performance degradation on regular services outside the scheme.

SLAs and business process outsourcing

As suppliers continue to expand the range of outsourced service offerings (as witnessed by the growth of business process outsourcing), the validity of the SLA as the primary control mechanism in the outsourcing arrangement is sometimes challenged. Regardless of the type of service being outsourced, the fact remains that the supplier is delivering a series of outputs which must be defined, measured and monitored. To this end the SLA is critical.

The difficulty with a business process arises where considerable interaction between buyer and supplier occurs before the supplier can deliver the final output. These 'interactions' themselves are critical to achieving the final output. Suppliers in particular should be keen to record these obligations as they often represent buyer commitments to the supplier which – if not fulfilled – will have an impact on the supplier's ability to deliver the final output. A typical example is where a supplier, in a payroll processing role, is obliged to make staff payments by a certain date. As part of the payroll process the buyer is required to sign off a list of staff a specified number of days before monthly payments can be made. Late sign-off by the buyer can result in late payroll payments by the supplier to buyer staff. The supplier must secure the buyer's commitment to sign off the list in time or else the supplier could be penalised for the late payroll payment even though the cause was beyond its control.

In some processes these buyer obligations can be numerous and make the SLA too long and unwieldy. Some suppliers have introduced OLAs (operating level agreements) which record the various commitments between buyer and supplier required to deliver the final output defined in the SLA. The OLA also contains measures and deadlines in relation to some or all of the obligations.

SLAs and partnership agreements

Some suppliers have been known to suggest that SLAs should not be required in 'partnership' agreements as the relationship is based on trust. Strong SLAs are perceived to be binding in nature, and their rigidity supposedly dampens the trust between the parties. Trust is not the issue. There is no reason why trust cannot develop from a relationship which is founded on the solid structure of a strong SLA. In fact, a successful relationship is more likely in this scenario.

In-house and outsourcing SLAs – the difference

Organisations which have already prepared SLAs between internal departments often query the validity of these agreements (often referred to as internal SLAs) for the purposes of outsourcing. In essence, if these internal SLAs define service outputs and the boundaries between internal supplier and buyer, they can, with some modification, be used for external outsourcing. The differences between these internal and external SLAs are typically:

- the internal agreement is not drafted in legal form – the external is;

- the internal SLA will refer to buyer and supplier in specific terms such as department names, job titles or even individual names. The external agreement will refer only to the separate buyer and supplier entities;

- the internal SLA may use a considerable amount of company jargon including department names and abbreviations. In the external SLA all such terms will be defined in the contract;

- in internal SLAs the boundary between services is quite often more vague than in external agreements.

How long does it take to create an SLA?

There is no clear answer to this question. It is a function of:

- the number of services which are transferred to the supplier;

- the number of user groups which receive these services;

- the number of service management staff drafting the SLAs;

- the number of users assisting the service management staff with the development, and their availability;

- the maturity of the user community (or at least the representatives) and their understanding of their requirements;

- the extent to which legal advisers are involved from an early stage;

- the process applied to draft the SLA and the management of the process;

- the level of commitment of both supplier and buyer organisations to the drafting process.

Typically SLAs seem to take between three and 12 months to create. Poor process and lack of staff availability seem to be the main reasons that the process is time consuming.

Service pricing in SLAs

The issue of pricing services is complex and is dealt with in detail in Chapter 7.

Summary

The SLA has several roles in the life of an outsourcing deal. The most important must be as a control mechanism to assist the monitoring of supplier and buyer operational commitments. The effectiveness of the control mechanism is partially a function of the strength of the SLA. A strong SLA defines clearly *what* the service delivers, *when* it delivers it and *where* it delivers it to. It should not be allowed to deviate into a description of *how* the service is delivered.

9

Manage the outsourcing contract effectively

Introduction

The phases of selecting a supplier and negotiating a contract are often such a drain on the outsourcing team that there is a sense that the outsourcing deal is over once the contract is signed. In fact, it is just beginning and these earlier phases were merely preparing the buyer and supplier for the next five, seven or ten years together.

The decision maker is now faced with one of the most important challenges: to ensure that the deal is correctly managed to deliver the expected outsourcing benefits and ensure the risk of failure is kept to a minimum.

In order to extract maximum benefit from the outsourcing deal, the buyer must manage its deal with the supplier in a structured and co-ordinated way. Without structure and co-ordination, the buyer risks trying to operate a deal where management processes are unclear, firefighting becomes the norm, decisions are made in isolation and thus are often contradictory, and the buyer incurs unnecessary cost.

To manage the outsourcing deal the decision maker must appoint a dedicated contract management team. This chapter examines the role of contract management in an outsourcing deal. It describes the skills required in a contract management team and the size of the team, and comments on the place for contract management in today's organisation.

The role of contract management

The objective of contract management is to leverage every possible benefit for the buyer from the outsourcing deal and also to ensure that the buyer is not subjected to any unnecessary risks as a result of the way in which the contract is operated. For example, where the contract entitles the buyer to an upgrade, or 'refresh', of its existing technology, contract management should ensure that this upgrade is consistent with the organisation's technological requirements for the years ahead.

Contract management involves both day-to-day operational activities, such as monitoring service performance or ordering new services, and less frequent (but regular) management activities, such as assessing the progress of the outsourcing deal and briefing senior management on various deal options as they arise.

> **Contract Management**
> **versus**
> **Service Management**
> **versus**
> **Relationship Management**
>
> These three terms are often used to denote the management function which the buyer puts in charge of its outsourcing deal. The difficulty is that they are used by different people to mean different things. For the purposes of this book, *contract management* is an umbrella term which encapsulates all aspects of managing an outsourcing deal, including managing the service(s) received from the supplier and the relationship with the supplier.

The contract management team has two primary interfaces, one with the service users (whether buyer employees, clients or other third parties) and one with the supplier. The contract management team will play different roles for its different customers. For the service users its role will include understanding their requirements as the deal progresses, matching these against the organisation's strategy and assessing overall achievement of the objectives of the deal. In relation to the supplier, the contract management team will need to review performance, request new services and manage charging and compensation mechanisms.

The reader, however, must also be quite clear as to what is outside the role of contract management. For instance, it does not involve the control of the delivery of services from supplier to users. The role of the user is to requisition and use services. This means that the contract management team should take a much more 'hands off' approach to service delivery and some contract management teams have difficulty with this. Their concern is that if they do not control service delivery, users are likely to make huge demands and the supplier will fulfil the demands and charge accordingly. The example usually cited is a typical personal computer outsourcing deal where, once it is signed, the users order the latest personal computers and the first the contract management team knows about it is when the supplier submits a large invoice for the equipment.

> **Contract Management and SLAs**
>
> A significant part of the contract management role is to monitor the performance of service delivery, discuss and implement alterations to the services and ensure that all the services which were contracted for are delivered. The services are described in the SLA, along with respective performance measures. Changes to services should be recorded in the SLA.

Issues such as these can be resolved by ensuring, first, that the contract management team authorise supplier payments; second, that payment will not be authorised if the item purchased was not on a list or in a catalogue of 'allowable items'; and third, that the contract management team charge back service charges to the user departments.

The desire to control service delivery that contract management teams are often made up of some of those who managed – and controlled – the original function or process before it was outsourced. However, if they continue to try to control the day-to-day operation of the services, they are most likely to ignore the more pivotal contract management tasks such as monitoring and requisitioning services. In addition adopting a controlling role ultimately only serves as a bottleneck in the service delivery mechanism – thus denying the organisation the real benefits of outsourcing.

There is a concern today that organisations which outsource to bring new practices and skills into their organisations will fail to get these benefits if the contract management team is not capable of delivering these benefits. It is therefore important that the contract management team understand that some of its roles are new and are not an extrapolation of its former function or process management role, and that new skills will probably be required to perform the new role.

The service management roles

There are essentially six main roles that contract management needs to address. They are to:

- **Procure**
  - one-off services (e.g. disaster recovery);
  - changes to existing services (e.g. extending hours of service coverage);
  - new services (e.g. adding Internet services to a personal computer deal);
  - projects (e.g. to make computer systems millennium compliant);
  - solutions to business problems (e.g. in an IT outsourcing deal using new technology to assist the buyer reach a broader client base).

- **Develop**
  - service delivery procedures and processes;
  - service delivery standards;
  - new user requirements;
  - risk reduction strategies (e.g. project roll-out to the user community).

- **Monitor**
  - performance of the supplier through service reporting, benchmarking user feedback;
  - supplier invoices;
  - progress of projects;
  - changes to services;
  - standards (e.g. ISO9001 implementation);
  - potential impact on the outsourcing deal resulting from large buyer or supplier organisational changes, e.g. acquisition, divestment;
  - risks to the organisation as a result of the outsourcing deal with this supplier (e.g. financial stability of the supplier);
  - financial performance of the deal against expectations modelled at the outset of the deal.

- **Implement**
  - changes to the outsourcing contract and specifically the service level agreements;
  - service delivery procedures and processes, including procurement procedures, to reduce the day-to-day involvement of the contract management team.

- **Facilitate**
  - transfer of knowledge from supplier to buyer and vice versa;
  - exchange of ideas between buyer and supplier solution groups;
  - new changes within the buyer organisation.

- **Communicate**
  - listen to users (e.g. outlining requirements, feedback about services);
  - present progress reports on the deal to senior management;
  - discuss service performance with suppliers;
  - develop new services opportunities with suppliers;
  - listen to supplier feedback;
  - advise senior management, users and suppliers;
  - attend supplier presentations on its capabilities;
  - provide to the supplier, on a regular basis, relevant information regarding the buyer organisation such as restructurings.

This list of activities and tasks is not exhaustive and can be quite extensive. Also, the degree to which these activities and tasks will be needed in a specific outsourcing deal almost certainly depends on the type of outsourcing deal (in particular where it is on the risk/reward scale – *see* Figure 1.1), the stage the deal has reached and the maturity of both supplier and buyer organisations in terms of their outsourcing experience.

Where the deal is an FM or operational type of outsourcing (*see* Figure 1.1) a strong monitoring role will be required. As one moves to the right-hand side of the scale there is a greater need to facilitate knowledge transfer and understand more about how the supplier's and buyer's capabilities can be harnessed together to add value to both organisations.

Service Calendar

A service calendar lists all key events in the outsourcing contract such as:

1   year end (or other key dates);

2   one-off service calls (e.g. disaster recovery tests);

3   service reporting dates;

4   service monitoring meetings.

Suppliers often prepare a service calendar. Buyers should make sure they take a copy.

The stage that an outsourcing deal has reached also affects the relative need for contract management.

- The first six months are usually a bedding-in time for the new supplier, the service users, the contract management team and the transferred employees – this is sometimes referred to as the *incubation* period. The supplier and contract management team need to work closely to develop solutions to service delivery problems and to carefully monitor service delivery. During this period the supplier is learning about its new client. Communication is focused on day-to-day issues and there may be very few orders or requests for new services.

- Towards the end of the first year the supplier is *operating* the services more confidently. Service monitoring becomes more regular and formal. Service delivery procedures and processes are refined. The contract management team is implementing more service changes to the contract, specifically the SLA, and is looking to the supplier to optimise services in cost and quality terms, especially where best-practice models were specified in the contract.

- At the 18- to 24-month mark in the deal the supplier is operating the services, incorporating service changes and undertaking small to medium-size service *enhancement* projects. The supplier and buyer are probably communicating more about their individual capabilities, requirements and problems and are exploring possible new projects. The contract management team spends more time and resources facilitating discussions about new projects and solutions, followed by planning and implementation sessions. Again, the contract management team must monitor carefully fledgling projects.

- Finally, as the outsourcing deal matures, the parties become more experienced at developing ideas and solutions and converting them into new projects, rolling out those projects and transferring them into operational services. The contract management team will monitor the larger risk and reward structures flowing from these new projects.

(The time line in the description of these phases may alter for many reasons and is therefore difficult to determine precisely. Thus the reader should treat the timings as indicative only.)

The degree to which both buyer and supplier will be capable of working together to effectively deliver services, both existing and new, will be partly a function of their experience to date of operating this type of deal with similar expected benefits. It is normally the case that the supplier is more experienced than the buyer – a fact borne out by the apparent frustration with their buyers often described by some suppliers.

Contract management skills and expertise

So far this chapter has described the objectives of contract management and has identified the primary roles required of a contract management team to fulfil those objectives. In order to play these roles effectively the contract management team needs specific skills and expertise.

Team and individual skills and expertise

Team skills and expertise

Table 9.1 shows the team skills and expertise which a typical contract management team should consider developing.

Table 9.1
Typical contract management team skills and expertise

Team expertise
Outsourcing (supplier selection, contract negotiation)
Performance measurement
Service management
Understanding of buyer organisation, its business and markets
Understanding of supplier organisation, its business and its capability
Outsourced function area (e.g. data centre, accounts receivable process)

Team skills
Negotiation (in dealing with both supplier and users to match user needs with supplier capability within the framework of the contract)
Financial modelling
Performance benchmarking
Conflict resolution and facilitation
Solution development (idea generation, conversion of idea to solution, solution viability assessment, conversion of solution to project)
Programme management of multiple projects, including risk assessments
Communication (with all stakeholders)
Risk assessment

As mentioned above, the values encompassed by a contract management team can contribute significantly to the effectiveness of the team. Teams whose values include openness, teamworking, collaboration and learning and which do not allocate blame but are receptive to new suggestions and ideas will be better able to deal with the challenges of contract management than those which try to apportion blame, criticise and seek to justify their position by controlling the supplier–buyer relationship.

Creation of a contract management team with positive values is not likely to happen by osmosis. For this reason – and because time is never plentiful in outsourcing transactions, particularly at the beginning of the deal – it is recommended that the buyer uses its human resource department or external advisers to help develop the type of team it requires to manage its outsourcing contract effectively and thereafter regularly coach that team in improving itself.

Individual skills, expertise and experience

The team skills and expertise described above are derived either from individual attributes or a mixing of individuals' attributes. Table 9.2 identifies the skills and expertise required of the individual team members.

Table 9.2
Skills and expertise required of individual members of the contract management team

Individual expertise, skill and experience

Outsourcing transactions, finance, legal, project management, negotiation

Benchmarking, functional (e.g. IT)

Functional (e.g. IT, finance, HR), help-desks, SLAs, negotiation, communication

General management in buyer organisation, business administration

Experience of working in business areas which will receive the outsourced services

Functional (e.g. IT, finance, HR), both in operations and management

Negotiation, outsourcing transactions

Project management, risk management, project implementation experience, change management skills

Training and experience in customer management, help-desk experience

Experience of product development

Programme planning, risk management, programme monitoring

Communications training, listening skills

Facilitating groups, training in facilitation

Team working

It should be the case that some of the skills, expertise and experience required to manage an outsourcing contract were present in the outsourcing project team which selected the supplier and drafted and negotiated the contract, including the SLA. It is recommended that some of this team be retained to form the contract management team. It is not, however, recommended that all members of the outsourcing project team be retained since some of their skills will no longer be required. In addition, the arduous contract negotiation phase may have reduced the effectiveness of some of the team at a most crucial stage of the outsourcing deal – the first six months.

Team reporting

The contract management team is generally flat in structure. This is usually born out of the fact that it comprises several experts or specialists who will need to get together with different team members and others to carry out their contract management tasks and activities. The team structure therefore needs to be quite fluid in order to facilitate the formation of many different work groups. For example, the team will need to have a sub-team responsible for such things as procuring new services.

The team should, however, nominate a team leader for co-ordination and reporting purposes. The team leader should report to the decision maker and to the senior manager responsible for outsourcing (*see* Chapter 4), where the organisation has appointed one.

Group size

The size of the contract management team depends on a number of factors such as:

- the complexity and volume of the services;
- the geographic spread of the services – both source and destination;
- the type of outsourcing deal (*see* Figure 1.1).

In addition the team size will also change during the life of the deal as new services and projects are commissioned. In the absence of a generally accepted method of calculating an optimal team size, a percentage of the number of people who transfer to the supplier can be used as a very rough guideline. The figure quoted is usually between 5 and 8 per cent. Figure 9.1 plots the approximate team size against the number of people transferring.

Figure 9.1
Size of contract management team

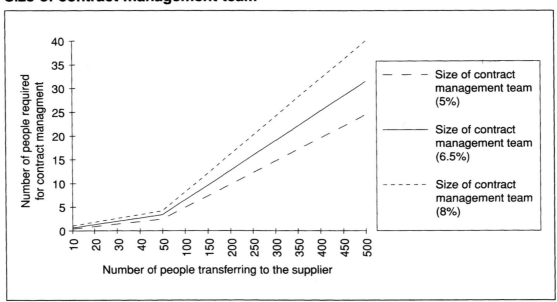

Contract management measurement

As stated at the beginning of this chapter, the objective of the contract management team is to leverage as much benefit as possible from the outsourcing contract for the buyer organisation. Since the team is directly or indirectly involved in almost every aspect of service delivery, the most appropriate measures which should be applied to the team are those used to measure the supplier. Typical supplier measures which could also be applied to the contract management team include the number of issues resolved in a defined time, the number of successful business projects and scores on user feedback forms.

Contract management as a career

Contract management, in the context of outsourcing deals, is a relatively new concept for many organisations. For organisations which will become more and more reliant on outsourced services it is a competence that will increase in importance. As organisations discover that effective contract management can enable them to derive benefits from outsourcing that their competitors cannot, the importance of contract management will increase exponentially.

It is imperative that attention is focused on developing this competency as it is a buyer's gateway to the competencies of many other organisations through outsourcing. To facilitate the growth of contract management skills decision makers need to make this role a viable career path in their organisations. Decision makers will also need to define the contract management skills and expertise that they want and make these part of contract management career development. External training assistance will probably be required in developing and delivering training programmes and in building and coaching contract management teams.

Summary

An effective contract management competence is critical for organisations wishing to maximise the benefits that they reap from their outsourcing deals. An effective contract management team will focus on facilitating rather than controlling the delivery of the service to the buyer.

The winners in outsourcing will unquestionably be those who develop an outsourcing competence and make that competence a central part of their organisation.

Five things to do after signing a deal

1 Appoint a contract manager and contract management team.

2 Prepare a service calendar (*see* description on p. 111).

3 Identify key supplier contacts (such as the contract manager).

4 Set out the process for service procurement, changes, one-off requests.

5 Schedule user and supplier meetings to monitor and improve services.

10

Be prepared for contract termination

Introduction

As the end of an outsourcing contract approaches, both buyer and supplier will need to decide whether to renew (or extend) their contract for an additional period or whether to go their separate ways. This is quite distinct from the situation where one or both of the parties terminates the contract during its lifetime because, for instance, the other party is in breach.

The buyer and supplier that choose to continue together will spend time before the termination date negotiating the terms of the new or extended contract. Most of the processes and issues set out in Chapter 6 apply equally in this situation.

Where the parties choose to go their separate ways, whether at the end of the contracted period or as a result of one of them terminating the contract prematurely, they will enter a phase in the outsourcing lifecycle called 'termination' or 'transition out'. The transition-out phase usually begins several months before the contract end date, or transition date and ends sometime after this date – ideally when the buyer is satisfied that the transition was successful. During the transition-out phase the buyer will make arrangements so that services continue to be provided to its organisation (whether by the old supplier, a new supplier or in house) after the date on which the current contract ends. The risks to the buyer in this phase are formidable. This chapter examines these risks and the factors which influence them. It outlines a generic process to assist the buyer organise the transition. Finally, a series of recommendations is set out in relation to specific transition-out risks.

Typical Reasons for Termination

- Termination for convenience (usually buyer only) which may be exercised if there is a change in strategic direction which removes the benefits of the outsourcing deal.
- Breach of contract – the contract usually defines 'breach' to include:
  - persistently poor supplier performance;
  - buyer refusing to pay service charge invoices.
- Supplier insolvency.
- Change of control in supplier or buyer organisations.

Transition risks

The principal risk which transition poses to a buyer is the possibility of catastrophic business failure as a result of disruption to the services which are to be transitioned. Staff unease and disruptive transition activities such as supplier retendering all threaten the performance of the outsourced services. In addition, once the transition date arrives the buyer will need to ensure that it has control of the services in their new home – whether in house or with a new supplier. Loss of service control means loss of control of the outsourced function. Where the outsourced function is a finance function this can be a significant problem for the organisation's senior management and the auditors.

The buyer will also be concerned with the financial impact of the transition. Potentially there are several hidden costs associated with the transition process and the buyer will want to minimise and control these as far as possible.

Finally, a risk which all decision makers should be aware of during the transition phase is one of capability. Is the buyer organisation capable of transitioning the services to another supplier or back in house and, if the latter, has it the ability to manage and operate them?

Factors affecting transition risks

The extent to which the above risks are a threat to a buyer organisation will depend on a number of different factors. The list in Table 10.1 is not exhaustive but is intended to provide the decision maker with a framework against which he or she can assess the organisation's exposure to transition risks. A low- and high-risk scenario is described for each issue listed in the table.

Table 10.1
Factors affecting transition risks

Issue	Low risk	High risk
Supplier–buyer relationship	• Where both parties mutually agree to terminate the outsourcing agreement the probability of mutual co-operation and crucial supplier assistance during transition is higher.	• One of the parties terminates the contract. Potential disagreement over the reason for termination can create a poor relationship between the parties. • Transition risk rises with the possibility of the parties being obstructive and uncooperative.

Issue	Low risk	High risk
Access to information	• Buyer has access to the information necessary to make transition decisions. • The supplier has maintained a register of buyer service related staff and associated assets, including hardware and software. • Recent SLA, process and procedural documentation and service performance information is available.	• Buyer lacks information necessary to transfer services. Records have not been maintained or are not available. • Buyer is unable to assess which assets will transfer and which assets will need to be replaced.
Transition option chosen	• The services transfer to a single organisation (and destination) – whether in house or to another supplier. • With in-house transition, the inbound services fit easily into the current buyer structure.	• Services are fragmented and transferred to in-house and third-party supplier or multiple suppliers, leading to high risk of service disruption or failure to allocate responsibility for specific services which may slip through the cracks.
Availability of skills	• There is a strong in-house or third-party transition team (in terms of quantity and quality of skill and expertise) to manage the transfer.	• Poor transition team. Time divided between several tasks.
Service integration	• The components (staff, assets) of the buyer's services within the supplier organisation are clearly separable from the rest of the supplier organisation, for example services are provided to the supplier's other clients from a separate facility.	• Services have been integrated by supplier with other clients' services. • Several supplier clients share supplier staff and assets such as computer hardware and software.
Contractual termination rights	• The buyer has contractual rights to: – receive from the supplier its service assets; – interim transition services from the supplier; – return of SLA, process and other service provision documentation.	• The buyer's termination rights in the contract are inadequate.
Length of transition period	• The buyer has sufficient time to decide transition options and transfer services.	• The buyer does not have ample time to transfer the services before the transition date.

A transition process

The transition of outsourced services from a supplier to another third party or back to the buyer is a lengthy process which comprises a number of key steps. The process set out below assumes that the buyer is taking the lead role throughout, both in terms of task management and execution. The buyer may, however, choose to pay the supplier to carry out some or all of the steps. It should be remembered that the supplier will also have a considerable amount of its own transfer preparation work to do during the transition phase. Assistance may also be provided by a consultancy, law firm or another supplier. The steps are as follows:

Step 1: Decide which options are available to the buyer for relocating its services

This stage involves gathering information on the composition of the buyer's services, assessing whether an in-house or third-party capability exists to provide them and which – based on potential benefits and risks – should be used. The buyer may wish to fragment the services by placing some with one or more third parties while the remainder will be taken back in house. All of the buyer's options must be assessed against a background of the risks described above to ensure that the desired option is achievable. A buyer may discover during this step that it is too risky to transition and may enter discussions with its existing supplier – although there is a always a risk that the supplier does not want to extend the life of the deal.

Step 2: Design the transition process

The buyer will need to design and plan a transition project to achieve the option chosen in Step 1. The project should be staffed by a team similar in structure and skills to that described in Chapter 3. The option to be followed will determine the team's activities. Where, for example, the buyer chooses to transition to a third party, the team may need to dedicate resources to finding a new supplier (as set out in Chapters 5 and 6). It is imperative that the team involves all the key players when planning the transition, i.e. supplier, in-house functions (including HR), other suppliers and lawyers.

Step 3: Implement the transition plan

Once planning is finished and plans have been agreed by the various parties involved, the transition team will implement the plan. Some of the activities to be carried out are:

- resolving staff issues;
- staff communications;
- tendering for a new supplier;
- contracting with the new supplier;
- transferring contracts and licences currently with the supplier.

During this step a seemingly infinite number of issues may arise for resolution. In addition a number of key relationships must be managed to ensure effective co-ordination of tasks. These relationships might include the existing supplier, a new supplier, business heads in the buyer organisation, the buyer's auditors and third-party asset suppliers.

Step 4: Monitor the transition

This process happens partially in parallel to Step 3. The intention is to stand back from the transition implementation, assess issues and risks which might arise and proactively resolve them. Additionally, from the transition date onwards, it will be very important to monitor the progress of the transitioned services.

Transition recommendations

There are a number of issues which may arise in a transition project which pose a threat to its success. These issues and risks are described below, together with specific recommendations to mitigate them.

Consider a transition agreement

There are several points which the supplier and buyer will want to agree at the outset of the transition phase. Although some of the issues might be dealt with in the original outsourcing contract, it is unlikely that all of the provisions which the buyer needs now were anticipated when the contract was signed. Additionally, some of the original contract terms might need to be changed. For these reasons the buyer and supplier should consider a transition agreement. This agreement would not replace the original outsourcing contract but its terms should supersede some of those in the original contract. Also, new terms should be added to deal with previously unforeseen issues. Ultimately, this agreement provides a framework for the co-operation of both parties during this difficult phase.

Some of the issues which both parties might like to consider for inclusion in the transition agreement are as follows:

- *Changes to the transition date.* Where the transition date conflicts with a key business date or a key milestone of another critical project such as a move from one facility to another, the buyer might wish to override the original date. Also, where the buyer feels that the time remaining before the transition date is too short and represents a significant transition project risk, it may wish to push the date back. Finally, it may be more advantageous for the buyer to transition different services at different dates. However, suppliers will often resist such a change to the original deal unless offered suitable financial rewards.

- *Additional service requirements.* The buyer may require a number of one-off services from the supplier during this phase, such as assistance with staff announcements and allowing access by a third-party bidder to supplier managers for information-gathering purposes and document production. It is important to agree these now so that both parties understand the resource and cost implications of these requirements. It is also useful if supplier charges are agreed as this phase is very resource intensive and can be very costly for the buyer.

- *Future of assets and personnel.* Though the future of the assets which the supplier uses to provide the buyer's services should largely have been provided for in the original contract, the buyer and supplier might need to review these provisions and strengthen them (for instance to deal with changes to the existing asset base over the life of the deal). Both parties will need to agree whether TUPE applies to the transfer of those supplier employees who currently provide the buyer's services. Where employees provide services for several of the supplier's clients this can be a thorny issue. The aim of the buyer is to secure everything it requires to provide the services in the future.

- *Transition liabilities and indemnities.* The supplier will be keen to ensure that its liabilities to the buyer end when the transfer occurs. It may also seek an indemnity from the buyer against such things as post-transition employee or third-party actions. The buyer should obtain reciprocal protection from the supplier. This area will be the subject of much debate in any outsourcing transition – particularly among lawyers.

- *Third-party contact.* Until the transition date, the supplier owns and manages the buyer's services. The buyer must usually seek permission from the supplier if a third party wishes access to them. The rules of engagement for these visits should be set out in the termination contract. The buyer will want to ensure that it has a mechanism to allow third parties access to the assets, particularly the documentation.

- *Work shadowing.* Where there are employees who will not transition to the buyer, the buyer will want those employees to pass on their knowledge and expertise regarding the provision of the services to the buyer or the new service provider. This is best done by work shadowing the supplier employees. This must be carried out in a controlled way to ensure that the supplier staff are not disrupted when providing the services but, at the same time, the necessary knowledge transfer occurs.

- *Visibility of employee movements.* This issue is considered again later in this chapter but it is worth mentioning here. The greatest risk to the buyer during transition is that the resources it requires to operate the services do not transfer to the buyer or nominated third party (for the reasons explained later). Critical to the buyer's ability to pre-empt resource shortage situations is receiving knowledge from the supplier with regard to staff movements. The supplier is often reluctant to provide this information but it would assist the buyer considerably during transition.

These are just an indication of the sort of issues to be covered but it is likely that there will be other issues specific to the deal which also need to be resolved.

Make cost provisions

A buyer that is transferring services to another supplier or back in house will need to make provision for a number of costs which may arise during the transition phase. These costs include the following:

- *Assets.* Assets which are part of the transferring services will need to be purchased or leased from the supplier (or on the open market). Some assets which the supplier uses to provide a service may be shared with other clients of the supplier, for example the property. In this case the supplier will probably not relinquish the asset. The buyer will have to purchase or lease that asset or find another supplier which has spare capacity on a similar asset.

- *Contractors.* It may be necessary to hire contractors during the transition phase to fill resource vacancies.

- *Staff.* With the current volatility in the job market in many countries, especially in IT skills, it is often necessary to offer incentives to entice employees to transfer with the services. This topic is dealt with in more detail in the next section. Additionally it is often the case that holiday and overtime accrued while working for the supplier are transferred with the employees to the new supplier or back to the buyer; either way the buyer will pay for it.

- *Assistance.* Buyers are often understaffed during a transition. Their own staff need to concentrate on ongoing service provision. In this case the buyer may seek the assistance of another supplier or consultancy. Usually legal advice is also required.

- *Supplier charges.* As stated above, the buyer will need to commission some one-off services from the supplier, which can be costly. The provisions in the original contract may secure some of these services at no additional charge. Where no provisions were made, everything is extra.

Do not underestimate HR issues

The key to an effective transition is that the people who operate the services transfer with the services. The intellectual capital of those involved in day-to-day service provision cannot be easily or quickly replaced. The loss of this intellectual capital increases the risk of service disruption or failure during and after the transition phase.

The largest proportion of the effort in a transition project will most likely be focused on assessing resource requirements, implementing resource transfers and resolving human resource issues. Some of the issues to think about are as follows:

Transferring staff

The buyer and supplier will identify those staff who will potentially be transferred with the services. The parties will take a view on whether TUPE applies. As previously mentioned, where personnel provide services for several clients of the supplier this can be a difficult issue. One way to approach it is for all employees who spend more than an agreed threshold of time on the buyer services to transfer. Typically the threshold agreed will tend to be between 50 and 100 per cent. However, this is a complex area which will need to be determined on a case by case basis and legal advice should be obtained.

Where TUPE does apply, all of the supplier employees associated with the undertaking will automatically transfer, although this will usually be documented in an offer letter. Employees do, however, have the option to refuse to transfer. Sometimes suppliers are not keen to transfer all the staff and wish to 'cherry pick' and steps should be taken to avoid this happening.

Where TUPE does not apply, the parties will agree who will transfer – usually after a considerable amount of negotiating as each seeks to get the best staff. What is essential to remember is that ultimately it is the employee who decides whether he or she wants to transfer. The buyer must pay close attention to who is not transferring to decide what skills replacement is necessary.

Staff communication

Once a buyer and supplier agree the staff who will be given the opportunity to transfer, the supplier will make an announcement to these staff. Ideally the buyer should be present at these announcements, armed with a prepared statement which should allay any fears that staff may have regarding their future. However, the buyer's presence is the supplier's choice as it is still the employer of the staff. Often at this point it is still not clear whether staff will transfer to the buyer or to another supplier. Future announcement dates should be scheduled to keep staff up to date. Regular consultation should also be scheduled so that staff can voice issues and concerns. They will decide whether they transfer or not. If the buyer wants them it will need to work hard to win their confidence.

Staff retention

The buyer will need to offer the transferring staff new terms of employment. Where TUPE applies, the terms of employment cannot be less favourable than they were previously. However, there is an issue as to how much better the new terms must be to entice the staff to transfer with the services. The staff may be good targets for the supplier or other organisations to poach. They may also simply want to remain with the supplier. Incentives (such as bonuses) are often used to ensure staff retention in these circumstances, but it is advised that bonuses should not be paid until several months after the transfer when the services have stabilised. Buyers would also be well advised to keep in close contact with local recruitment agencies so that they can fill skills shortfalls at short notice. Finally, buyers should bear their current staff in mind. Where outsourced staff are returning to the buyer's organisation on better terms than the current staff (possibly including bonus schemes) the existing buyer staff might feel like second-class citizens, leading to lack of motivation and poor performance.

Have an escalation procedure

There are generally many issues which will only be resolved with buyer and supplier co-operating. However, emotions on both sides can run very high at times during the transition phase, hindering communication and collaboration between the parties, particularly where the outsourcing relationship has been a lengthy one. Both parties must ensure that a process is in place to transcend these skirmishes and ensure that communication between buyer and supplier – which is vital to the success of the transition – does not break down. Regular structured meetings between the senior management of both parties will help effect good communications. Both parties should focus on progress to date and on the expedition of any issues which still need to be resolved.

Build a project team

The buyer will require a dedicated project team to run the transition project. A similar team structure to that described in Chapter 3 is recommended.

Monitor risks

The project team should monitor closely and carefully transition risks as they arise. These must be reported regularly to the key decision makers and to the meetings of the senior management recommended above.

Test transitioning services

The simple recommendation here is to test transferring services wherever possible rather than opting for a 'big bang' approach. Flicking the switch for the first time on the big night is a high-risk strategy which is unlikely to work!

Summary

A recent survey by KPMG[1] suggested that the outsourcing contracts of almost 60 per cent of those polled would end within two years of the time they were surveyed. Of those, one-third expected to renew with their existing supplier, the rest would terminate, with a 50/50 split between those intending to take the services back in house and those intending to transfer to another supplier. A cost-effective and smooth service transition is crucial to ensure that these buyers continue to reap the benefits of outsourcing.

---

1. *The Maturing of Outsourcing*, London: KPMG, 1997.

11

Conclusion

The popularity of outsourcing as a tool to implement corporate strategy is expected to continue to grow steadily over the coming years. Outsourcing will also change as organisations look increasingly to outsource suppliers to assist them to compete in their business markets. With this in mind, organisations can be expected to look for deals which provide more business benefits and for suppliers which are capable of taking on more service development and delivery risks. Buyers will have to pay more for this.

As many first-generation outsourcing contracts come to an end buyers will re-evaluate their deals and will decide whether or not to continue to renew their outsourcing contracts with the same supplier. Whether they choose to remain with their existing supplier or seek another, they can be expected to have much higher expectations of their second-generation suppliers. This in turn can be expected to force some of the more generalist suppliers to refocus their attentions on fewer activities, possibly requiring them to renegotiate the scope of some of their client deals.

As the pressure on outsourcing to deliver more in a shorter time frame increases, the success of many outsourcing deals will be measured by the shortest time it takes to get into a deal and harness the benefit from it. The outsourcing process as it stands may be too lengthy for both parties and may need to change. However, getting to a deal more quickly may require both parties to forego meticulous deal preparation and lengthy negotiation. Both buyers and suppliers will need to improve their understanding of the risks to which such compromises will expose them and whether they are acceptable or not.

Truly global outsourcings are still in their infancy. There are already numerous international deals where a single supplier provides a service to a buyer in many countries, but where the deal is none the less managed at a country or regional level. However, in these types of deal, the true advantages of global service supply, where the supplier employs the competencies of different geographic and functional parts of its organisation, are not fully realised. As many buyers themselves are facing the challenges of globalisation they will look to their suppliers to demonstate their global capability.

Finally, organisations which expect to harness outsourcing effectively must include the management of their outsourcing deals as one of their critical competencies. This will require both additional investment for some organisations and the recognition of outsourcing as a key business activity within the organisation.

Glossary

Buyer	Purchaser of outsourced services.
Contract management	The function of managing the outsourcing deal.
Due diligence	A process of ascertaining the identity, quantity and quality of assets to be transferred from buyer to supplier.
FM	Facilities Management.
Function	Support activity in an organisation including IT, human resources, finance (payroll, accounts receivable, asset management).
IT	Information Technology.
ITT	Invitation To Tender.
OLA	An Operating Level Agreement is a subordinate document to an SLA which describes specific buyer and supplier commitments to each other.
RFI	Request For Information.
RFP	Request For Proposal.
RPI	Retail Price Index.
SLA	A Service Level Agreement is a document which describes the services provided by the supplier to the buyer.
Supplier	Provider of outsourced services.
TUPE	Transfer of Undertakings (Protection of Employment) Regulations 1981.
Users	Business units within the buyer organisation to whom outsourced services are provided.